THIS MY LOVE ISN'T

Goodbye

PAUL MCCOY

Author: Paul McCoy

Printed in the United States.

ISBN: 978-1943393923

CONTENT

DESIRE AND INTENT

I have been blessed to be able to visit the Fertile Crescent twice in my lifetime. Those who are not Muslims or history enthusiasts may ask, "Why would anyone want to go to Iraq?"

If I'm going to be honest, as a child I had no desire to go to this place. I was raised as a Christian and I was told that modern-day Iraq was Babylon, and that only bad things happened in that place. From the Christian perspective, the children of Israel were kidnapped and forced to go to Babylon. The enemies of God resided in that place.

This is my background; this is what I was taught as a child. Growing up, the area was part of what is known as the Fertile Crescent, the place where many people believed civilization and mankind originated. It is also the place where many in the religious world believed the Antichrist would emerge. After all, this was the Middle East.

When I was about eight years old, the United States had a conflict with Iraq's neighbor, Iran. We heard about the hostage situation in Iran, and watched as the Iran-Iraq war unfolded. This conflict lasted for about ten years and introduced the world to Saddam. During that conflict, I didn't know anyone who would entertain visiting this war-inflicted land. That conflict lasted until I graduated high school.

In 1990, I became a student at Savannah State University. As I mentioned earlier, I was raised in a Christian family; my maternal grandfather and mother are ordained Christian ministers. I was always a believer in God, but I questioned some of the beliefs held in Christianity.

For example, I didn't believe in the original sin: I questioned how a God could be loving and punish all of humanity for a mistake that was made by two individuals. I also never understood the concept of the trinity. I questioned and pondered these tenets my whole life and was never given an answer that made sense to me.

I never contemplated becoming an atheist or leaving religion altogether, but I knew that I did not and could not in good conscience remain a believer in those ideologies. I remember trying to find the answers that I was looking for. I started going to different churches, Bible studies and revivals, because I always loved God, but I just couldn't give up on faith without doing my due diligence to find those answers. I finally found the answers I was looking for in the unlikeliest places. I met a guy in college who was a Muslim convert and we began to converse, or better yet, debate about religion. We went back and forth for hours using the Bible as our point of reference in trying to reach truth. The guy gave me the book, "Is the Bible God's Word?" by Ahmed Dedat, and it confirmed everything that I believed. It debunked the concepts of

Trinity and original sin, and after reading it, I went home and had a conversation with my mother and informed her that I was no longer a Christian. On January 8, 1991, I made my declaration of faith: "I bear witness that there is no God but God (Allah) and I bear witness that Muhammad is the messenger of God!" I accepted Islam as my faith and I became a Muslim.

The excitement of taking this step to worship God in the way He intended human beings to worship Him was the greatest experience and choice I made in my life. At that point, I understood I had a religious obligation to go to the Middle East, to Saudi Arabia, and to perform the pilgrimage (Hajj) in the city of Mecca and visit the city where the Holy Prophet is buried, Medina.

I became acquainted with other converts, and we would meet and discuss how we would all complete this pilgrimage together. It was at that time that I developed a desire to go to that part of the world and I made my intention to make Hajj. In the religion of Islam, we are judged not only on our actions but also our intent. That intent and desire did not initially include making a trip to Iraq.

After becoming a Muslim, I learned about the different sects of Muslims practicing Islam. This was something new to me. In America, there is an organization called the Nation of Islam, made up of mostly African-Americans. To some, these individuals are not true practicing Muslims, but, for those of us who are familiar with them, in many cases they were our only reference to Islam and Muslims. There were also Orthodox Muslims who practiced a more standardized form of the religion.

As an African American, I was more familiar with the Nation of Islam than I was with Orthodox Muslims. After becoming a Muslim, I realized that there are many different sects. I also learned that many share the same beliefs, but there are some whose beliefs are totally different. I started learning the differences between the major sects of the religion, mainly the Sunnis and the Shia.

My search led me into a world of research and debate. All I truly wanted was to find the true path to God. At that point in my life, I was discovering the traditions of the Prophet, and those traditions became my main source of study and research.

I read, watched, and eventually, participated in debates but as a neutral participant. My stance was that people should not divide faith and fight each another for what I deemed to be petty differences. Oddly enough, it was during the Holy Month of Ramadan, in the year that I converted to Islam, that I began to read the Holy Quran with the commentary. While reading the commentary, I began learning more about Islamic history.

As a new convert, I learned about the Holy Prophet Muhammad, his companions, and his wives, and if I'm not mistaken, I learned all of that information in that order. It was only after I began to debate and take a closer look at history, that I began to see the importance of the prophet's family, i.e., the Ahl al-Bayt. The commentary of the Holy Quran explained their significance and shed light on what happened to them after the departure of the Holy Prophet. I was a sponge; I read anything I could get my hands-on concerning Islam.

My best friend at the time was reading a book, and he enjoyed it so much that he purchased a case of the books. The book was titled, "Then I Was Guided" by Muhammad al-Tajani; he gave me a copy as a gift. After reading the book and discussing the arguments and evidences presented in it, I became a Shia Muslim. After becoming Shia, my best friend and I would often talk about going overseas to study Islam, become great scholars, and reach the point of being jurists, i.e., Ayatollah[1]. This awakened a desire in me, I had made my decision - my intent, and sought to study in Iran. At the time, Iran was the only place I knew of in which I could pursue Shia Islamic Studies.

I read as many books as I could find, and talked to as many people as I could about the religion. That was the full extent of my Islamic life at that time. In reading the history and finally finding out about what happened to the Prophet's family, I couldn't help but to mourn for them. When I became a Muslim, and more

---

[1] Ayatollah (translit. ᵓāyatu llāh "Sign of God") or ayatullah is a high-ranking Usuli Twelver Shīah cleric. Those who carry the title are experts in Islamic studies, such as jurisprudence, Quran reading and philosophy, and usually teach in Islamic seminaries. The next-lower clerical rank is Hujjat al-Islam-wal-Muslimeen.

importantly, when I became a Shia Muslim, I did not live around people who were engrossed in the cultural norms and traditions of Shia Islam.

Although I became a Shia and read about what happened in Karbala[2], Iraq during the month of Muharram[3], I had no idea that people were having programs or performing reenactments of

the events that took place on the Euphrates River[4]. No one that I knew ever expressed interest in visiting the place where the massacre of

---

[2] Karbala also Kerbala, is a city in central Iraq, located about 100 km (62 mi) southwest of Baghdad, and a few miles east of Lake Milh. Karbala is the capital of Karbala Governorate, and has an estimated population of 700,000 people (2015).

The city, best known as the location of the Battle of Karbala in 680 CE, or the Mosques of Imam Husayn and Abbas, is considered a holy city for Shi'ite Muslims.

[3] Muḥarram is the first month of the Islamic calendar. It is one of the four sacred months of the year during which warfare is forbidden. It is held to be the second-holiest month, after the Holy Month of Ramaḍān. Since the Islamic calendar is a lunar calendar, Muharram moves from year to year when compared with the Gregorian calendar. The tenth day of Muharram is known as the Day of Ashura, part of the Mourning of Muharram for Shia Muslims. Shia Muslims mourn the death of Imam Husayn ibn ʿAlī and his family, honoring the martyrs by prayer and abstinence from joyous events. Shia Muslims do not fast on the 10th of Muharram, but will not eat or drink until zawal (noon) to show their sympathy with Imam Husayn. In addition, there is an important visitation (ziyarat) book, the Ziyarat Ashura about Husayn ibn Ali. In the Shia sect, it is popular to read this ziyarat on this day.

[4] The Euphrates is the longest and one of the most historically important rivers of Western Asia. Together with the Tigris, it is one of the two defining rivers of Mesopotamia (the "Land between the Rivers"). Originating in eastern Turkey, the Euphrates flows through Syria and Iraq to join the Tigris in the Shatt al-Arab, which empties into the Persian Gulf.

the Prophet's grandson Imam Husayn, his family, and companions took place.

In Savannah, Georgia, where I was living, there was no Shia mosque or sheikh (religious leader). The few of us who decided to tread this path had to rely on one another with our limited knowledge and resources. Believe me, the resources were scarce, but our resourcefulness was boundless. We only had a few books in our possession, so we decided to write to the publishers of the books we had and we began receiving books from all over the world to increase our Islamic knowledge. Not only did we write to publishers, we traveled to different places including Houston and New York to buy books. While traveling, I attended a Shia mosque for the first time in Queens, New York.

My best friend, who was originally from New York, left Savannah and returned home, and I later moved to New York so that I could learn more about Islam. While there, I heard something new pertaining to going to Hajj[5]. I

_____

[5] The Hajj is an annual Islamic pilgrimage to Mecca, Saudi Arabia, the holiest city for Muslims, and a mandatory religious duty for Muslims that must be carried out at least once in their lifetime by all adult Muslims who are physically and financially capable of undertaking the journey, and can support their family during their absence.

heard the term 'ziyarat'[6] for the first time. A group of African-Americans from the mosque I was attending in Brooklyn, New York, were planning to go to Hajj and few other places that I wasn't interested in going to at the time, but they mentioned ziyarat.

While in New York, I came to learn more and continued to read many books, but I still did not understand the true culture of Shia Islam. It wasn't until I moved to Atlanta, Georgia and became a part of a Shia Muslim community where Muharram programs were held, that I really began to see and learn the Shia culture.

It was good and bad, because most of the programs that I attended were not in English. When I decided to go and learn Islam from a teacher in Atlanta, I finally began to understand the nuances and purpose of why things were done and the importance of having a connection with the Imams of Ahl al-Bayt. I understood why people at the end of Friday prayer would

---

[6] In Islam, ziyara(h) or ziyarat is a form of pilgrimage to sites associated with Muhammad, his family members and descendants (including the Shīa Imāms), his companions and other venerated figures in Islam such as the prophets, and Islamic scholars. Sites of pilgrimage include mosques, graves, battlefields, mountains, and caves.

Ziyārat can also refer to a form of supplication made by the Shia, in which they send salutations and greetings to the Holy Prophet Muhammad and his family.

stand and recite things in the Arabic language that I did not initially understand. I knew that they were names and I knew who these names represented, but I didn't know the significance of doing what we were doing at the time. I was now being taught about having a connection and relationship with these individuals whose names were being recited. I was told that if at all possible, I should travel to visit the shrines of these individuals and perform ziyarat.

My teacher was from Iraq. He talked about his country and he would visit home periodically. I noticed that he would mostly go home during Arbaeen (the 40th), which is the period of mourning on the fortieth day after the martyrdom of Imam Husayn. I started putting the puzzle together, and understood more of what I has been reading and studying for years about the culture, because I was around someone who was willing to share it with me. Having gone through the process of transforming information into knowledge and having the ability to apply that knowledge was empowering.

Now the desire and the intent to go to Iraq was burning in my soul. I wanted to visit the places where the saints of God made the ultimate sacrifice, to ensure that those of us who are alive 1400 years later would have the ability to worship Him in the way that He intended, is nothing less than a miracle. While writing this, I realized that it took over a decade from the time that I accepted Islam as my way of life, to making my intent and having the desire to visit the saints of God in Iraq.

THE INVITATION

I found that many believers have expressed their desire and intent to visit the saints of God. They have asked the fortunate ones who have gone for visitation before them to pray while they were there to please have our Lord, the Most High, grant them the ability and permission to be able to visit His saints.

I mean, it seems like it's a simple task: you buy a ticket, get a visa, reserve your rooms, and just go; doesn't it sound simple?

I was told that there were many who wanted to make the trip to be with the most beloved of God. I imagined all the millions who desired to visit and pay homage, and were unable to, during the occupation of Iraq. While learning more about the culture, I was also told that having the ability to go to Hajj and ziyarat came with an invitation from the Most High. I was cautioned that just because the invite is given and accepted, it is not a sign of you being a good believer. I have had the misfortune of knowing people who have gone to Hajj and visited the saints of God who are no longer on the path. They have left the religion.

The invitation comes with a responsibility and my best friend, who I mentioned earlier, said to me when he came back from Hajj and visitation,

> *It's like Satan takes his little satans off of you when you go to these places, and he puts his big satans on you, because your act of worship and obedience should have increased your faith, so he assigns bigger satans on you.*

At that point, I was yearning to visit the most beloved of God. However, I did not have the means to go to ziyarat. I used to listen to people who made the journey, and who had the experience of going to Iraq; my eyes would fill with tears, and my heart would yearn to be in those places, and in the presence of the people they were talking about. No one talked about the accommodation, no one talked about the food, no one talked about the typical things that people talked about when they go on vacation.

Those fortunate ones who made the trip only talked about the feelings of peace and of joy, and of being honored to be among the fortunate and blessed ones and to have had communion with God's most beloved. The language, the authenticity, the genuineness of their love and appreciation for being allowed to make the visitation only served to increase my desire to visit my Lord's most beloved.

In 2013, more than a decade after I made my intent to go to Iraq, I received an invitation. I was in California and had just completed a series of lectures for the month of Muharram. At the time, I was sitting around with a group of believers from the center where I was lecturing, and we were talking about Iraq. I was the only one in the room who had never been and some of the people who were there were making plans to go within the coming weeks. I remember expressing how I wished that I were able to join them, and asked them, which is customary, to pray that I am extended this divine invitation to make the journey someday.

I was asked, "You really want to go?"

My answer was, "Of course, I want to go."

I was asked if I had a passport, and my reply was, "Yes, I have a passport."

At that moment, my heart was pounding, but I had to temper my excitement, because these questions were great, but I knew that I didn't have the means to go. I was told to send my information and a photocopy of my passport to the cousin of one of the attendees and we would go from there. I told the gentleman that I really didn't think that I would have the funds to go and he told me that all I would need was spending money and that he would take care of the rest. That brother was true to his word and I was able to make my first trip to visit the saints of the Almighty.

I don't know what it is about being with the believers during and after the Month of Muharram. Well, let me think about that for a second. There's nothing like being with the believers and discussing going to visit Imam Husayn. I found myself in a conversation like that in London, England. I was talking about my experience the first time I went to Iraq, and I expressed my desire and intentions to go back at any time the opportunity presented itself. My financial situation had not changed, and when I made that statement, I knew that I did not have the means to go. The believers being who they are, informed me that there would be a trip coming soon and that if I wanted to go, they would make it possible for me to go. I leapt at the opportunity, and in December of 2017, I was fortunate and more importantly blessed with the opportunity to visit the saints of God for a second time. All praises belong to God.

THE CHALLENGES

The joy I experienced receiving those invitations was incredible, but I was facing a challenge. I am a family man and as such, I was responsible and accountable for others. Beaming with excitement, I went to tell my wife about my upcoming trip, but all I could see in her eyes was concern, not excitement. She expressed that she was happy that I was given the opportunity to go to Iraq, but from the perspective of someone who has not experienced that yearning desire, why would anyone want to go to Iraq? Sure,

Saddam was gone, but the country still had foreign troops. It wasn't necessarily the safest place in the world and the media was constantly reporting on attacks and suicide bombers in the country. Convincing her that I would be ok traveling to this war-torn country was my first challenge. Next, I had my children and my extended family who really didn't want me to go, but could clearly see how much I wanted it. In the end, they understood my overwhelming desire and blessed my trip. Prior to my departure, they all joined me in a prayer asking God to protect me during my journey.

For my first trip, my wife and one of my daughters came to the airport with me to bid me farewell. I was okay until it was time for me to go to the terminal. I remember looking at my daughter, who was thirteen at the time, and how tightly she grabbed and hugged me. It was like a movie: we were both crying in the middle of the airport as if we were never going to see one another again. At that moment, I recognized that my biggest challenge was in front of me. My daughter was truly thinking that "my dad may never come home." That's a lot to swallow! It makes you think about your mortality, for the first time I didn't think about the benefit of going, but I began to think about what was going to happen to my family if something were to happen to me! The moment of clarity, that "we belong to God and to God we must all return", became apparent.

It didn't matter if I was in Atlanta, Georgia, U.S.A. or the Holy City of Najaf, Iraq; the one who had control over my life will always have control over my life, and geographical location doesn't matter. I let them know that God had only used me as a vessel to care for them, but that I had faith in Him and He would always provide for them. I pulled myself away from my family after we prayed and I made my way to the terminal.

During my second journey, my biggest challenge was my mother. My mother is a Christian preacher and she had been watching some Evangelical ministers and their topic of discussion was the Middle East. My mother knew my financial situation, and she said to me that she and my stepfather would pay for my expenses for a month if I did not go to Iraq. I found myself in a conundrum. I had found a job, but it would not begin until January of 2018, and because I hadn't been working a traditional job, my finances were not what they should have been.

On the one hand, I was going to Iraq and there was not going to be any financial compensation for the trip; my greatest incentive was the blessing of being able to visit God's saints. A foundation funded my trip, and I know if I had told them that I needed to back out, they would not have been happy, but they would have understood, so I had that option. See, you don't know my mother. Well, she's my mother and she has a great deal of influence over me. We are taught in Islam to always honor our parents, and the mother has one of the highest positions over us. The last thing that I would ever want to do would be to disappoint my mother. I had to pray and it was a struggle. The fact that I was not in a good place financially, and my mother's willingness to help me out until I started my job, put me in a peculiar place. However, after talking and praying about the situation, my mother said, "Put your trust in God and he will direct your path."

All the challenges were resolved, and once again, I was on my way to be with my Lord's most beloved.

Well, that was the plan, at least. I figured if I could convince my mother that it was okay for me to go, then there was no way I was going to have any type of hiccups when it came to me making this trip. I was wrong!

I faced a great challenge on the day that I was scheduled to leave. I arrived at the airport early to check my bags, and I was ready to go. There was a young man from the Atlanta community who was also going on the trip, I saw when I walked in to the airport. The young man's uncle is a good friend of mine, and he asked me to look after him while we were away. He was having complications with his ticket and it took customer service a long time to sort it out. I waited for him and the delay caused us to miss our flight. It's in these moments that you can do one of two things: you can either begin to pray and put your faith in God that everything is going to be okay, or you can feel dejected, give up, and say that this was a sign that you were not supposed to go. I did the former!

I walked to the gate and the workers at the gate were looking through the flight schedules to see when we could be put on a different flight. We had a connecting flight to Philadelphia. I wasn't really worried, because I felt like if we were able to take another flight to Philadelphia, and make our connecting flight, we would be okay, but if we weren't going to be able to make the connecting flight in Philadelphia, it wouldn't make sense for us to leave Atlanta. Let me tell you, blessings come in a lot of different forms, and I truly believe that I had the help of the twelfth imam on that day.

It just so happened that a young lady and her son were scheduled to take the same flight we were scheduled on. The young lady was rerouted and separated from her son, who had special needs. The son was on the plane and the plane had already left the terminal. This lady made a fuss, explaining that her child had special needs and had to have medication at certain times, and that he did not have his medication with him because the medication was with her. The young man who was there with me was saying, "Man let's just go." I told him to have patience. After this lady argued with the people, they had the plane come back to the terminal. I know that the plane coming back was an absolute miracle. What was more miraculous was that once the flight log is completed and turned in, you're not supposed to add people to the flight. That didn't happen: favor was on our side and we were able to catch that flight, and we arrived in Philadelphia on time and were able to make our connecting flight!

Yet another challenge was presented when I arrived in Philadelphia. There was an issue with my ticket and I thought that I wouldn't be able to get on the plane going from Philadelphia to Doha, Qatar. Time was ticking, everyone was boarding, and I was thinking, "Could this really be happening to me right now?"

But I understood that it was a trial and a test. We were promised that we would have trials and tests, so I was up to the challenge. They were able to figure out and resolve what the problem was with my ticket, and I was able to board the plane. At that point, I was finally on my way to be with my Lord's most beloved. Again, I prematurely thought that my challenges were behind me but, I still had more to come!

THE ARRIVAL

In 2013, my arrival into Iraq was scary and amazing at the same time. It was amazing because I was arriving at a place I had been dreaming of for years, and it was scary because while we were landing, I looked out the window and it looked like there was a sandstorm and no one could see the runway. It was also scary because after we cleared customs we had to go through checkpoints. Now for those of you who are not familiar with checkpoints, allow me to help you understand what they are.

Remember when we would go to the airport and we would hear, "The security threat level is orange"? In Iraq, the security level was red! There were insurgents, suicide bombers, and a whole lot of bad people who were making life in Iraq difficult for everyone. In order to protect the people, armed guards were placed in certain areas and it was their job to stop people and to check them and their belongings, to make sure that they weren't carrying anything that could harm others.

I want to paint a picture here. Think about walking out of the airport, going to your vehicle, loading your luggage and leaving the airport like we do in the States. That didn't happen in Iraq. Before we left the parking area, we had to pass through a checkpoint. That was the first one and before we made it out of the airport, we passed through three more security checkpoints. At one of those checkpoints, we had to exit the vehicle, our bags were taken and checked, and it felt like it took forever. I'm from the hood, I am an inner-city kid, and dangerous situations don't bother me, but I was seriously afraid, because all of these guys had machine guns and although they did not brandish them or point them in our faces, all of them had their fingers on the triggers. That's enough to give anyone an uneasy feeling.

After leaving the checkpoint, we were driving through Iraq, and it looked like something from the news. Bridges were taken out, half buildings were standing, and I promise you, before we got to the main area of town, I passed by someone in a box being pulled by a donkey, someone riding a horse, someone riding a bike, someone riding a motorcycle, trucks, and how could I forget the Humvees with soldiers also holding machine guns?

I remember thinking to myself, did I make the right decision?

So, we continued on our ride, while I was looking around with my eyes wide open, wondering what I had got myself into, and all of a sudden, we came to a stop. I looked around to see why we stopped. I was hoping that it was not another security checkpoint. I was told that we had arrived at our destination, and that our bags would be taken to our hotel. People I didn't know were taking our things from the van while I was thinking to myself, "Surely we are not where we are supposed to be, because I didn't see anything!"

Again, I'm a city boy, so I was looking for places to duck and hide at if something was to go bad and there was nothing, no place for shelter. Now we were on foot, walking, and I had no idea where I was going. We were approaching a place that seemed like a guard shack. I recall thinking to myself, "Here we go again with the machine guns," but as I got closer, my eyes began to rise and what I saw in the distance was a golden dome. We had reached the Shrine of Imam Ali!

Upon seeing the shrine, all fear that I had immediately disappeared. I felt a sense of peace that I had never felt in my life. I said, "Lord, if it is my time to go, allow me to go here in the shade of the brother of the Prophet."

We arrived on a Thursday which is the time for Dua Kumayl[7]. Here is how the supplication starts:

---

[7] Dua Kumayl (literally the Supplication of Kumayl) is a supplication famous among Shi'a for its perceived beauty and a traditional supplication in Shi'a. It is a Muslim spiritual practice. The Du'a is not an exclusively Shi'a dua, however, as none of its content is controversial among Shi'a and Sunni schools of thought. According to Allama Majlesi, Kumayl ibn Ziyad, a confidante of Ali ibn Abi Talib had attended an assembly in the Mosque at Basra which was addressed by Imam Ali, in the course of which, the night of the 15th of Sha'aban (a month) was mentioned.

بِسْمِ اللَّهِ الرَّحْمَنِ الرَّحِيمِ

In the Name of Allah, the All-merciful, the All-compassionate

اللَّهُمَّ إِنِّي أَسْأَلُكَ بِرَحْمَتِكَ الَّتِي وَسِعَتْ كُلَّ شَيْء

O' Allah, I ask You by Your mercy, which embraces all things

وَبِقُوَّتِكَ الَّتِي قَهَرْتَ بِهَا كُلَّ شَيْء

And by Your strength, through which You dominate all things,

وَخَضَعَ لَهَا كُلُّ شَيْء

And toward which all things are humble

It was surreal. I wasn't in a mosque, someone's house, an Islamic center, or listening online, I was at the Shrine of Imam Ali reciting this dua (supplication) and I could not stop the tears from falling down my face. This scary place, in my opinion, became the safest place on the planet. Elderly women would walk from the hotels unaccompanied to the shrine at all hours of the night, wanting to pray and beseech their

Lord, and they had no fear of anyone bothering them at all.

In 2017, I considered myself an old pro. After all, this was not my first rodeo and I figured I knew what to expect. But as I mentioned earlier, I prematurely thought that my challenges were over, I had no idea that I was about to encounter a new set of challenges.

When we arrived at the airport, we went to baggage claim and I noticed that my suitcase was missing. I had my book bag with me. In that bag was my computer, tablet, shoes, and a change of clothes. I was upset, because I couldn't find my suitcase. I looked and looked and it wasn't there. There was another young man whose suitcase didn't come in, so we had to file a claim. I sat my book bag down and asked one of the youths to hold it for me while I filled out a claim. Because it took a while to complete my claim, I had to ride to the hotel with other people and not with the group that I came in with.

At this point, my anxiety levels were extremely high, because I didn't have my suitcase. I was able to calm myself down, because I had a change of clothes in my book bag, and I was thinking that my suitcase would come in on a later flight and everything would be alright.

I arrived at the hotel and started asking about and looking for my book bag, because I gave it to the guys to take with them while I was filing a claim for my suitcase. Now that bag was also missing and no one had seen it. I could feel my anxiety levels rising. I tried to call the airport, but I wasn't able to talk to anyone. I contacted the guys who were responsible for the trip to see if I could go back to the airport to look for my book bag. They told me that they were at the airport, asked about the book bag and no one had seen it.

Now I was in Iraq with no clothes. All I had was my wallet, my phone with no charger and my passport. I began questioning everything. Should I have made this trip, how am I going to replace the things I lost, and am I even going to be able to go anywhere because I didn't have any clothing?

I found myself searching for answers but never losing faith. I stayed in my room on my first day in Iraq. The following day, everything changed.

MEETING THE SCHOLARS

In 2013, and again in 2017, I had the distinct honor and privilege of meeting three of the four Grand Ayatollahs of Iraq, Sayyid Ali al-Sistani, Sayyid Muhammad Saeed al-Hakim, Sheikh Mohamed al-Fayadh and Sheikh Bashir al-Najafi. To me, meeting these honorable scholars is comparable to Catholics meeting the Pope. These are individuals who dedicated their lives to learning about Islam, its laws, and how the laws apply. They are powerful and influential men, but you would never know that when you meet them, because they are so humble and always assume the position of servants of God. You would think that these individuals lived a life of opulence, in big castles decorated with expensive artwork and the best of everything around them. From what I observed, nothing could be further from the truth. These individuals live a conservative and humble life. Despite the enormity of their responsibilities, they take the time to speak with people who come to see them.

The first Grand Ayatollah I had the privilege of meeting was Sheikh Bashir al-Najafi. I met His Eminence after visiting Masjid Al Kufa. Again, this was scary. We arrived at his residence at night and when we got to his place, there were armed guards, again, with machine guns, and we had to be checked before entering his residence. I was expecting to enter a lavish place with deep carpets and luxurious seating. Rather, we walked in to find concrete walls, regular carpet, and simple pads on the floor for people to sit on. This was enough for me to feel at home. I didn't know what to expect from the Grand Ayatollah.

Was I going to meet someone who was super serious, no-nonsense, and who talked down to people? Well, I found out the type of individual Grand Ayatollah al-Najafi was soon after meeting him. He smiled when he entered the room, he was very cordial with people and took the time to answer everyone's questions. Some of the ways he answered the questions were really light-hearted and made you laugh, and at other times, when some in attendance were being a bit reckless, he addressed them in a loving, fatherly type of way. The advice he gave us was to continue learning our religion, and to share that knowledge with our communities. Before leaving, he gifted us his books and a precious stone to be used to make a ring.

The next Grand Ayatollah I had the honor of meeting was Sheikh Muhammad al-Fayadh. I was really looking forward to meeting him, because I met his son when he came to the States, and I was given the responsibility of reading his announcement in English to the Shia community in Atlanta. He was elated when I told him that I met his son, and that I had the opportunity to share his words with my community. I met him during the daytime, so security wasn't as stringent as it had been with Grand Ayatollah Sheikh Bashir al-Najafi. His eminence talked about the importance of education, and having the ability to discuss our faith with non-Muslims. Again, he had humble accommodation, but the hospitality was second to none. He served us, was attentive, and took the time to answer all of our questions until no one had any more questions to ask.

The last Grand Ayatollah I met in 2013 was His Eminence Sayyid Ali al-Sistani. This was indeed a great honor for me, because he is the individual that I hope to emulate. When I went to visit him, I was shy and overwhelmed. My visit with him was a little different, and although I was with a group, we had a personal conversation for about twenty to thirty minutes. What surprised me the most was his ability to speak with depth and accuracy about the conditions and political situation that was going on in the United States of America. At the time, there was a shooting incident in Connecticut, where an individual had shot and killed his mother in their home, and then went to a school and killed people there. He talked about gun control, he talked about the mindset of the people and he gave suggestions on what would be the best way to handle the situation. I never expected to hear this type of talk, or have this type of conversation with a man of his stature. When he spoke to me, he leaned in and he spoke very softly. He told me,

> *It is your responsibility to teach the people, it is your responsibility to guide, it is your responsibility to share the message of Islam with the people in your country. You have all the tools to do the job, so do it!*

That is a great big responsibility and one that I have never taken lightly.

In 2017, what I found apparent was his influence and leadership in his country. There was a tremendous change, and the climate had shifted when I returned for my second visit. This was largely due to Grand Ayatollah Sayyid Sistani's urging and insisting for the Iraqi people to free themselves from the oppression of Daesh (ISIS). He made it a culture to honor those who gave their lives to ensure the freedoms of the Iraqi public. Through different efforts, he ensured that the widows and orphans of those who lost their lives would be taken care of. He was able to help the Iraqi people see that they had the power within themselves to change their condition. As Muslims, one of the first things that we learn from the Quran is the verse that says, "Indeed, Allah will not change the condition of a people until they change what is in themselves."[8]

There were still checkpoints, but nowhere near as many as there had been the first time I came. The people looked happier, and the visitors who came to Holy Cities where the shrines are moved more confidently, knowing that the threat was not as great as it once was.

During my 2017 visit, I also had the opportunity to meet Grand Ayatollah, his eminence, Sayyid Muhammad Saeed al-Hakim. He was the only Grand Ayatollah that I didn't meet in 2013. That had been really disappointing to me, because I had the opportunity to meet his son when he came to Atlanta a few years before. Just like with the other scholars, we went to visit the Grand Ayatollah in his home and like the others, there was nothing extravagant about it. What I did like was that there were chairs, and he sat in a chair and there were those amongst us who had the

---

[8] The Holy Quran, 13:11

opportunity to sit in chairs too. When we visited the other Ayatollahs, we sat on the floor, which was traditional, and the only person who sat in a chair was the Ayatollah. Coming from a Western background, being able to sit in a chair for a long period of time was more appealing than doing the same on the floor.

The Grand Ayatollah gave us a speech that was more like a conversation, sharing with us how representatives from the Catholic Church and other Christian churches came to visit him, and the discussions they had pertaining to religion. The Grand Ayatollah explained Islam's solutions for some of the problems that the world faces. He was able to show that the solutions were viable, and those conversations led to an agreement regarding annual conferences.

What is really interesting about me meeting this great man is that I had been in Iraq for a full day and I hadn't gone anywhere, because I didn't have my clothes. While I was sitting around, beginning to feel sorry for myself, I had to remind myself that it doesn't matter to my Lord or His saints what I'm wearing: the fact that I was there meant that I needed to do what I went to do, and that was to worship my Lord and to commune with His most beloved. The morning before I met the Grand Ayatollah, I went to the shrine of Imam Ali and I had experienced a higher level of spirituality during my worship. I came back to the hotel and went with the group to visit the Grand Ayatollah. Upon reaching the Grand Ayatollah, I was told that my name had come up and I was being discussed amongst his group.

I was told that they were trying to find a way for me to come to Iraq to do some lecturing. All of this was new to me, and it was a welcome surprise. The representative of the Grand Ayatollah asked if I could meet with them the next day, when they would let me know what their plans were for me, if I was willing to assist them. While I was with the group visiting the Grand Ayatollah, I received a text with a picture letting me know that my suitcase came in, and that it would be at the hotel when I got back that night. What a blessing!

The next day, I was escorted to the office of the Grand Ayatollah, where I met with a group in charge of education. They were telling me about some of the issues the youth were facing. I was asked if I would go to some of the universities, Islamic learning centers, and meet with some of the professors of the universities while I was there. I spoke to the individuals who invited me to Iraq, and they let me know that they didn't have a problem with me volunteering my time with the Grand Ayatollah's office. I then agreed to volunteer with the representatives of Grand Ayatollah Sayyid al-Hakim to give lectures and speak to Iraqi college and university students.

VISITATION

I want to discuss the real reason for going to Iraq. When I came into the faith, my dreams and aspirations were to make it to the house of Allah, the Holy Kaaba in Mecca. For most Muslims, Hajj is the ultimate event, and Mecca is the ultimate destination, outside of heaven itself. I came to the understanding that there were other important places to visit after reading a passage from Imam Ali about certainty and true devotion. Imam Ali was asked, "Where would you rather be, in heaven or in a mosque praying worshipping God?" He answered, "I would rather be in a mosque."

He explained,

> *If I am in heaven, I am happy with myself,*
> *but if I am in the mosque worshipping my*
> *Lord, my Lord is happy with me.*

Amazing lines—who comes up with logic like this?

Unfortunately, I have not made it to Hajj, but I am truly hopeful and believing that one day soon, I will be invited to the House that Abraham and his son Ishmael built. Yes, I said invited again. In Islam, those of us who are practitioners are commanded to go to Hajj once in a lifetime, if we are financially able to go. I personally know many people who are financially able to go, who have the desire to go, but for a variety of reasons have not been able to go, reasons as simple as not being able to obtain a visa on time, to becoming ill just before leaving. I also know of people who had a sincere desire to go and didn't have means to pay for the Hajj, but were able to go because of the generosity of others from the blessings of God.

It was the invitation and the acceptance of it that allowed those individuals to make that unlikely trip to the house of God. In my case, my invitation to God's house has yet to be extended.

The Kaaba is the physical direction that we turn to as Muslims to pray. It is a physical reminder that there is a direction that we have in life that points us to our Lord. But how is it that we know anything about our Lord?

Our Lord, the Most High, in His infinite wisdom had sent mankind guides and examples to teach us about Him and the path that we need to tread in order to reach Him. God sent us Prophets and it was through them that we received revelation, understood what that revelation meant, and through them, we were guided on how to follow the revelation. We visit these individuals to remind ourselves of the mercy that our Lord extended to us through them. We remember the stories and relate them to others to encourage ourselves to do right in the face of difficulties. We visit them because our Lord, the Highest, used them as a means to reach us, and we, in return, use them as a means to reach our Lord. Many of the prophets referred to in the Jewish and Christian scriptures resided in and are buried in Iraq. Along with those prophets, some of the imams of Prophet Muhammad's household and their companions are also buried there.

There are some people who say that the Shia don't value Hajj as much as they value the ziyarat. Nothing could be further from the truth. We truly value Hajj, but it is very expensive, and there are limits to the number of people who are allowed to go there every year. Muslims are encouraged to go on Umrah[9] if Hajj is not available for them for whatever reason. During both the Hajj and Umrah, individuals make ziyarat or visitation. Hajj is visiting the House of God and the Prophet's mosque where he is also buried. Pilgrims also visit Jannat ul Baqi, where other imams and members of the Prophet's household are buried. Personally, the visitation takes on an additional role. Man was created having both a physical and spiritual existence, and if the Kaaba is the physical point that we turn to reach our Lord, then the Prophets and imams are our spiritual directions that we turn to

[9] The 'Umrah is an Islamic pilgrimage to Mecca, Hijaz, Saudi Arabia, performed by Muslims, that can be undertaken at any time of the year, in contrast to the Ḥajj which has specific dates according to the Islamic lunar calendar.

reach our Lord. We do this visitation to strengthen our relationship with those who guided us to our Lord and to strengthen our relationship with Him.

One thing that I will mention here is that before entering any of the shrines there, there is a ritual of asking for permission to enter. We make our intention clear, which is mainly to seek closeness to God. Entering these places, the main goal is to worship near those who worshipped God the best. It is to remember the sacrifices that those individuals made and the examples they gave to bring us closer to our creator.

أَشْهَدُ أَنْ لاَ إِلٰهَ إِلاَّ ٱللَّهُ

I bear witness that there is no god but Allah,

وَحْدَهُ لاَ شَرِيكَ لَهُ

alone without having any associate,

وَأَشْهَدُ أَنَّ مُحَمَّداً عَبْدُهُ وَرَسُولُهُ

and I bear witness that Muhammad is His servant and Messenger.

جَاءَ بِٱلْحَقّ مِنْ عِنْدِهِ وَصَدَّقَ ٱلْمُرْسَلِينَ

He has conveyed the truth from Him and verified the (past) Messengers.

اَلسَّلَامُ عَلَيْكَ يَا رَسُولَ ٱللَّهِ

Peace be upon you, O Messenger of Allah!

اَلسَّلَامُ عَلَيْكَ يَا حَبِيبَ ٱللَّهِ وَخِيَرَتَهُ مِنْ خَلْقِهِ

Peace be upon you, O most-beloved of Allah and best of His beings!

اَلسَّلَامُ عَلَى أَمِيرِ ٱلْمُؤْمِنِينَ

Peace be upon the Commander of the Faithful:

عَبْدِ ٱللَّهِ وَأَخِي رَسُولِ ٱللَّهِ

the servant of Allah and the brother of Allah's Messenger.

يَا مَوْلَايَ يَا أَمِيرَ ٱلْمُؤْمِنِينَ

O master, O Commander of the Faithful!

عَبْدُكَ وَٱبْنُ عَبْدِكَ وَٱبْنُ أَمَتِكَ

I, your slave and the son of your slave and your bondmaid,

جَاءَكَ مُسْتَجِيراً بِذِمَّتِكَ

have come to you seeking the refuge of your protection,

قَاصِداً إِلَىٰ حَرَمِكَ

directing to your shrine,

مُتَوَجِّهاً إِلَىٰ مَقَامِكَ

turning my face toward your place,

مُتَوَسِّلاً إِلَى ٱللَّهِ تَعَالَىٰ بِكَ

and begging Almighty Allah in your name.

االدْخُلُ يَا مَوْلاَيَ

May I enter, O master?

االدْخُلُ يَا امِيرَ ٱلْمُؤْمِنِينَ

May I enter, O Commander of the Faithful?

االدْخُلُ يَا حُجَّةَ ٱللَّهِ

May I enter, O argument of Allah?

االدْخُلُ يَا امِينَ ٱللَّهِ

May I enter, O trustee of Allah?

االدْخُلُ يَا مَلاَئِكَةَ ٱللَّهِ ٱلْمُقِيمِينَ فِي هٰذَا ٱلْمَشْهَدِ

May I enter, O angels of Allah who reside in this shrine?

يَا مَوْلاَيَ اتَاذَنُ لِي بِٱلدُّخُولِ

O master, may you permit me to enter

افْضَلَ مَا اِذِنْتَ لاحَدٍ مِنْ اوْلِيَائِكَ

in the best way of permission, you have ever given to any of your devotees?

فَإِنْ لَمْ اكُنْ لَهُ اهْلاَ فَانْتَ اهْلٌ لِذٰلِكَ

If I am too little to deserve your permission, then You are too exalted to deprive me of it...

I am an American, African-American to be specific, and I would have never thought that I would kiss a door, or cry, or rub materials on them in hopes of taking some of the blessings from them, but going through the doors, I did. The blessings don't come from the materials, but the fact that they are a part of the structures that housed God's most beloved makes them a blessing. I went there knowing what many people do when they go to the shrines, I purchased prayer stones, and asked God to bless those who prayed on them in the shrine, and I asked God to bless specific people and donated those prayer stones in their names, and on their behalf.

THE HOLY CITIES OF THE SHRINES

Iraq is a large country. The shrines we visited are located in different cities throughout the country. There are a few things that I would like to share that I learned about in a few of these cities when discussing them.

THE HOLY CITY OF NAJAF[10]

By far, my favorite shrine city is the Holy City of Najaf. After he strategically arranged the bodies of the martyrs in Karbala, Imam al-Sajad was asked where he was going once his task was completed. The imam stated that he was going to Najaf. When asked why, he stated, "Do you not know that you receive blessings for sleeping in Najaf?"

If Imam Ali was the seed that was planted in the soil, what has that seed produced? That seed has produced scholarship of the highest order. The Holy City of Najaf is one of the premier seats of Islamic knowledge in the world. It is home to some of the oldest continuous Shia seminaries. Students from all over the world go there to learn Islamic knowledge, and go back to their homes and other places to spread the good news of Islam.

Many people start their journey to the Holy City of Karbala from the Holy City of Najaf. They first visit Imam Ali before going to visit the

---

[10] Najaf is a city in central-south Iraq about 160 km (100 mi) south of Baghdad. Its estimated population in 2013 was 1,000,000 people. It is the capital of Najaf Governorate. It is widely considered the third holiest city of Shia Islam, the Shi'ite world's spiritual capital.

shrine of Imam Husyan and the martyrs of Karbala. At the end of the mourning period for the martyrs of the forty days (Arbaeen) following the anniversary date of the killing of Imam Husayn, many of the pilgrims leave Karbala and go to Najaf, and remain there until after the death anniversary of our beloved Prophet Muhammad. The Holy City of Najaf has become an important city in Iraq and has its own international airport. It is the home of four of the greatest scholars in Shia Islam. It has the world's largest cemetery, Wadi-us-Salaam[11] (the Valley of Peace) and Prophets Saleh and Hud are buried there.

People from all over the world flock to Najaf, to be near the one individual Prophet Muhammad proclaimed as his brother, the one who the Prophet said was the soul of himself, the one who willingly volunteered to sleep in the bed of the Prophet when there were people looking to kill him, the one who was the first of the people to accept Muhammad. His seed has produced great fruits and great benefits for mankind.

---

[11] Wadi-us-Salaam ('Valley of Peace') is an Islamic cemetery, located in the Shia holy city of Najaf, Iraq. It is the largest cemetery in the world. The cemetery covers 1,485.5 acres (601.16 ha; 6.01 km2; 2.32 sq mi) and contains tens of millions of bodies. It also attracts millions of pilgrims annually.

Normally, when thinking about a Third-World nation, especially one with a tumultuous history like Iraq, one doesn't necessarily think about technology, learning, and individuals putting positive things out into the world.

While in Najaf, I found that the individuals who are in charge of the seminaries are doing just that. They have built beautiful academies, and have placed the best technology within them to ensure that those who attend school there are afforded the opportunity to receive the best education. I visited many seminaries, but the one that stood out the most to me is the one that is ran by al-Khoei[12] Foundation. I entered into this beautiful building that almost seems out of place, because it's just as modern as any building that you would find in any major city in the U.S.

The common string between all of the seminaries in the Holy City of Najaf is that Islam contains the answers to all the world's problems.

What they are doing that is so amazing to me is that they are inviting the brightest individuals

---

[12] Grand Aytollah Sayyid Abu al-Qasim al-Khoei (November 19, 1899 – August 8, 1992) was a Shia cleric and one of the most influential Twelver Shia Islamic scholars (Grand Aytollahs). He was the spiritual leader of much of the Shia world until his death in 1992. He was succeeded by Grand Aytohhal Sayyid Ali al-Sistani, his former student.

from around the world to come to the Holy City of Najaf with their secular educations and then supplementing that with Islamic education, so that they can go back to their places of origin and present Islam in a viable way that is acceptable and relatable to their people. Al-Khoei Foundation offers free education for any individual who wants to study there, but the individual has to commit to five years of study. To some people, that may seem extreme, but the reality is that if an individual wants to obtain a PhD, in most cases it takes at least five years. Furthermore, what is interesting is that they are not just inviting these individuals over to teach them Islam, they are also inviting them over to learn about the sciences and information that they bring with them to improve and increase the levels of knowledge that is being taught in these facilities.

All of the cities of the holy shrines have a vibe, a feeling about them. While I was in Najaf, I felt the vibe of spiritual perfection and I don't think that was a coincidence. The brother of the Holy Prophet is there! There is much to say about a man who, when he first opened his eyes, saw the eyes of the Holy Prophet Muhammad, and the same man when Prophet Muhammad closed his eyes, whose eyes were the last eyes the Holy Prophet saw.

The sheer magnitude of information that can be stated here about Imam Ali is altogether mind-boggling. The suffering that this man endured, to have his right usurped from him. The kindness that he showed his enemies. The justice that he gave to others when so many had been so unjust to him.

Earlier, I talked about my challenges, but who was more challenged than Imam Ali? The feeling I have when I am in Najaf is one of complete peace. Life has us so busy that we forget that we will all return to our Lord. Imam Ali always thought about his meeting with the Almighty, and the highlight of Imam Ali's life came when he was fatally struck and he made the proclamation, "By the Lord of the Kaaba, I have succeeded!"

He understood that the whole purpose of life is to prepare oneself for the life to come.

While in Najaf, many people take the opportunity to go to Kufa. I found Kufa to be very spiritual and sad. Going to visit al-Kufa

Mosque[13] requires a whole day because of the sheer amount of stations dedicated to the Prophets who came through the area and worshipped there. While walking through the Mosque, every couple of feet, you come to an area where a particular prophet, servant of God, or martyr was known to worship, and we receive blessings for worshiping God in the same place. There are many stations, and after performing the recommended acts of worship, I particularly felt like I went through a deep spiritual cleansing.

At the end of going through all of those stations, you get to the place where Imam Ali made his night prayers. To stand in that same location, and to pray there, cannot be described by my words. To see where the imam was struck made me cry. The real sadness was going to the house of Imam Ali, seeing how it was configured and knowing where his family members slept, which made the imam more human to me, more than anything I've ever read about him. I am a visual person, and in my mind's eye, I could see when

---

[13] The Great Mosque of Kufa, or Masjid al-Kūfa, or Masjid al-Mu'azam/al-A'azam located in Kūfa, Iraq, is one of the earliest and holiest surviving mosques in the world. The mosque, built in the 7th century, contains the remains of Muslim ibn 'Aqīl - first cousin of Imām Husayn ibn 'Alī, his companion Hānī ibn 'Urwa, and the revolutionary Mukhtār al-Thaqafī.

they brought Imam Ali from the mosque, after he was struck, to his home. I can see where his children tended to him. I can feel the anguish that the young Abu Fadl Al-Abbas felt watching his father die.

The journey to this place attaches you to these individuals, and to know what they went through because they said "God is my Lord, and I am going to enjoin the right and forbid the wrong", brings you closer to your Lord. To know that those who came before us did not just give lip service to Islam, but that they are the ones who actually paid the ultimate price in establishing and maintaining it, inspires the true believers. Before leaving al-Kufa Mosque, I had the opportunity to get water from a well that was hand dug by Imam Ali. This again served as a reminder to me that he was a real man, who did real work, who had a real family, who delivered the real message of Islam, and who reached the stage of martyrdom for doing so.

Not too far from al-Kufa Mosque is al-Sahlah Mosque[14]. This place, like al-Kufa Mosque, has

---

[14] The Al-Sahlah Mosque or Masjid al-Sahlah is one of the primary significant mosques in the city of Kufa, Iraq. The mosque is of great importance to Shia Muslims, and it is believed that the mosque was initially established in Kufa as a

many stations dedicated for the prophets who came for worship. What is special about this place is that there is a station for the imam of the time, the great-great-grandson of the Holy Prophet Muhammad, who is known as al-Mahdi, al-Muntathar or the Awaited One. I had the honor of visiting this location twice, both on Tuesday evenings. This is significant, because the believers come to this place and recite a prayer called Dua Tawassul. In this prayer, the believers are asking the immaculate members of the Prophet's household for intercession to help them in this life and the one to come. This is how the supplication starts:

بِسْمِ ٱللَّهِ ٱلرَّحْمٰنِ ٱلرَّحِيمِ

اَللَّهُمَّ صَلِّ عَلَىٰ مُحَمَّدٍ وَآلِ مُحَمَّدٍ

In the name of Allah, the Beneficent, the Merciful.

O' Allah, (please do) send blessings to Muhammad and the Household of Muhammad,

---

neighborhood mosque for the followers of Ali, the early members of the Shia. The mosque is also said to be the future home of the twelfth Shia Imam al-Māhdi.

اَللَّهُمَّ إِنِّي اسالُكَ وَاتَوَجَّهُ إِلَيْكَ بِنَبِيِّكَ نَبِيِّ
ٱلرَّحْمَةِ، مُحَمَّدٍ صَلَّى ٱللَّهُ عَلَيْهِ وَآلِهِ

O' Allah, I beseech Thee, and We turn
towards Allah with your help, through Thy
Prophet, the Prophet of Mercy, Muhammad,
may Allah bless him and his Progeny, and
grant them peace.

يَا ابَا ٱلْقَاسِمِ يَا رَسُولَ ٱللَّهِ يَا إِمَامَ ٱلرَّحْمَةِ،
يَا سَيِّدَنَا وَمَوْلانَا، إِنَّا تَوَجَّهْنَا وَٱسْتَشْفَعْنَا،
وَتَوَسَّلْنَا بِكَ إِلَى ٱللَّهِ وَقَدَّمْنَاكَ بَيْنَ يَدَيْ
حَاجَاتِنَا، يَا وَجِيهاً عِنْدَ ٱللَّهِ إِشْفَعْ لَنَا عِنْدَ
ٱللَّهِ

O' Abul-Qasim, O' Messenger of Allah…
O' guide of mercy, O' intercessor of the
community, O' our chief, O' our master, we
turn towards Allah with your help, seek thy
intercession and advocacy before Allah, we
call upon you before [mentioning] our
requests [to Allah];

O' intimate of Allah, stand by us when
Allah sits in judgment over us.

We believe the twelfth in the line of imams from the Prophet's household will live and establish a righteous community. I am not trying to give a religious class here, but it is our belief that God will fill the Earth with justice through our twelfth imam. That imam is amongst us, but he is in a state of occultation. As Muslims, we all believe in Imam al-Mahdi, and that he will, with the permission of God, restore order to the world and complete the mission of the Prophet. Some people need to have a certain level of proof that this is not a story of legend. They need to know that this individual exists, and Masjid al-Sahlah serves as a reminder of that. The imam has a tangible place that we can go to and see where he will rule, and bring justice into the world. We have proof, and this is not just a farce. There's an actual place where he will be, to remind us of his existence and God's mercy towards us on Earth.

Previously, I mentioned the challenges that I faced. I experienced another challenge in the Holy City of Najaf. So, I mentioned that I lost my book bag when I first arrived in Najaf, which had my shoes in it, so I was walking around in slides. One night, I went to pray the evening prayers at the shrine, and I took off my shoes and left them by one of the doors leading into the place of prayer at the Shrine of Imam Ali. When I came out of the shrine, I looked for my shoes and they were gone. My initial thought was, "You're kidding me?" I can't believe that this would happen to me, and to make things worse. It was cold that night. I had to walk back to my hotel with no shoes on, but I didn't get upset about it. Instead I smiled and said to myself, "May Allah bless whoever has my shoes."

I was later told that if your shoes are taken away, it is a sign that you're going to return. I don't know if that is true or not, but I believe it with all of my heart. The greatest gift that I could receive is to be able to have another opportunity to be near God's most beloved!

THE HOLY CITY OF KARBALA[15]

The next city I visited was Karbala. During my first time going there, I stayed at a hotel right across the street from bab al-Qibla. Karbala

---

[15] Karbala is a city in central Iraq, located about 100 km (62 mi) southwest of Baghdad, and a few miles east of Lake Milh. Karbala is the capital of Karbala Governorate, and has an estimated population of 700,000 people (2015).

definitely has a different feel in comparison to Najaf. Let me interject here that as a believer, whenever you are in any Holy City that has a shrine, the shrine itself acts like a magnet that draws you in and compels you to worship. Of course, you're not worshipping the individuals, you are definitely worshipping God through the process of visiting the places. These are places that held the individuals who loved and worshipped God without compromise, and this puts the adequacy of your worship in perspective, it drives you to work harder to perfect your worship, to attain that proximity you are seeking to God in the hereafter. I remember lying in my bed and having to get up to go into the shrine and worship.

What I found interesting is that Karbala, like Najaf, did not exist before an imam was buried there. They did not become the urban areas we recognize today until people decided to settle in the vicinity of the holy tombs. Imam Husayn, along with his family and companions, did not set out to go to a land called Karbala. I had read about this place and the events that took place there for years. I had given lectures and cried about the events, and to have the opportunity to stand on those grounds and see where those battles took place, where the massacre took place, where the bodies of the slain were laid, is overwhelming and surreal. But the thing that is so great is the fact that our Lord, the Most High, used the scene of a horrific massacre and made it the place that has become the largest annual peaceful meeting place in the world. Millions of people descend on this place yearly to remember that massacre, and reflect on how it changed the world. It was through the bloodshed of Imam Husayn, his family and his companions, and by the mercy and permission of God, that we have Islam today.

I'm going to digress just a little bit here. You would think that the Iraqis would be bitter and cautious towards the visitors who flock to their country after their experience with war and

insurgency. There is no doubt in my mind that some of that does exist, but somehow, it seems to dissipate when people come to visit the Holy Shrine in the City of Karbala. On the death anniversary of Imam Husayn, and forty days after the death anniversary, millions of people descend to Iraq and go to Najaf, Baghdad, Basra and other places.

They prepare to walk from those places to Karbala to commemorate the death, tragedy, bravery, massacre, and most importantly, obedience of Imam Husayn and those who were with him. Again, citizens of this war-torn country, who have gone through unspeakable atrocities, show their love for Imam Husayn by lining up on the roadway, where people walk from the cities to Karbala, to feed and tend to those who are walking.

They make sure that they have water. If they are tired, they allow for them to sleep and get rest. These individuals would take the shoes of those who are walking to Imam Husayn, clean their shoes and rub their feet. Some people walk for more than two hundred miles to make it to Karbala. As mentioned before, this place calls you to worship.

It makes you appreciate the sacrifices others made to preserve the message that God has given to the world. I personally have not made the walk, but my intention by the grace and permission of God is to make that journey hopefully from Najaf to Karbala before the end

of my life. That within itself brings a unique type of spiritual gratification. I know other indigenous Americans who had the opportunity to walk, and to be on the side of the road helping those who are walking, and when they share their experiences, it seems otherworldly. You can see the glow on their faces as the tears stream down their cheeks, and it always seems as if they're looking out in the distance; but, I've come to understand where the mere mention of the experience takes one.

That look does not represent a mindless stare into the distance. It is a moment in which we are taken back to a place in our mind, so vivid, so real, it is as though we are transported to the past to re-experience the journey. It is as if we can feel the sand under our feet, and smell the perfume in our noses while giving our narratives of what happened while we were there. What may be the most beautiful part about all of this is that everyone that I know who has had this experience always talks about the burning desire they have of going back to visit those places.

My first time in Karbala, I had the opportunity to visit where the actual battle of Karbala took place about 1400 years ago. I went to the place that the Prophet's family were camped at. I saw how the tents were configured, and how the first tent housed Abu al-Fadl al-Abbas who was responsible for protecting the family. I saw the different chambers, and where the different family members were staying. I got completely overwhelmed when I thought about those individuals and their plight – especially the women and the children. These were real people in a real place, not just some story that we heard about. I walked through the tents and cried. I tried to put myself in their positions, but my mind would not allow me to deal with that type of trauma. Imagine that you are with fewer than two-hundred individuals, and you look across the landscape and you see an army of thousands who have assembled to kill you. What goes through your mind? You're running out of supplies and the babies in the camp need water, but you can't get to it—what goes through your mind?

I walked throughout the area and while walking, it was pointed out to me where the members of the Prophet's family and companions of Imam Husayn were martyred. Imagery is powerful, and being able to see it takes us to a different level. There is a fountain in Karbala, and in the fountain is a replica water satchel that represents the water satchel Abbas was trying to bring back to the children. To see where the arrows pierced the satchel, and imagine the water running from it in abundance, knowing that the Prophet's great-grandchildren didn't have the opportunity even to wet their lips with that water, is heart-wrenching. The water from the Euphrates was so close, yet not within reach. I read of all that inflicted Abbas when he attempted to obtain water for the children, how his hands were cut off, and to this day, there is a monument there that symbolizes that. I walked and I saw the places where the Prophet's great grandsons were murdered. Maybe the saddest place was where Imam Husayn's baby, Abdullah, also known as Ali Asghar, was martyred. There is a little crib in this place representing the six-month-old baby who became a casualty of war, because the enemies of God didn't want to obey His command.

The last place I went to while I was walking was to the station of Lady Zainab, the sister of Imam Husayn. This was a slightly elevated piece of land, similar to a small hill. It is said that she ran to this place so that she could increase her vantage point so she could see her brother fight in battle. It is one thing to hear or read about a tragic event, but to see it first hand is something altogether different. I love my siblings, and I don't know what I would do if I watched any of them being brutally murdered. The smile comes to my face, because I believe that the members of the Prophet's household understood more than anyone else the verse that says, "We belong to God and to God we must return." They were familiar with this, and it is almost like they adorned themselves with it, as if it were a coat. Having this knowledge did not deter them from faith in God; on the contrary, it actually increased their faith in God.

I walked over the bridge and saw the Euphrates River, with geese and ducks swimming in it. I went to the areas where the imams from the Prophet's household would stay while in Karbala, and worshipped in those areas. I went to the last place that many people say they saw the final imam, and prayed in that spot. I promise you, while I was standing there in prayer, it was as if there was a breeze that came through with a beautiful scent that I had never smelled before. When I finished praying, I walked around all the markets to see if I could find that scent. After searching for a while, I asked a man about the sweetest scent and he said to me that I smelled the fragrance of the imam of the time! I don't know if that was actually the case, but if it was, then that was a tremendous honor. If I am blessed to be alive when our imam returns, maybe I can get close enough to him to confirm that it was his fragrance.

Entering into the shrine of Imam Husayn is a humbling and sobering experience. The thing that's beautiful to me is that the companions of the imam, who died with him, have stations throughout the shrine. When we go to honor Imam Husayn, we don't just honor him, but we also honor his companions. The imam had some of the greatest companions and having them honored alongside the imam gives hope to all believers. This hope continues to resonate with me, and so many others, that doing the right thing, we too can be honored alongside the Imam of our Time.

When I went to Karbala for the first time, it was after Arbaeen, and many of the visitors who were there for that occasion had already left. So, I wasn't there with the massive crowds, and that created a sense of intimacy for me. I said each shrine had a feeling, and the feeling that I had while in Imam Husayns's Shrine was one of sadness. I was sad because the imam had watched his sons, brothers, nephews, and friends murdered. He was all alone and he hadn't done anything to deserve being murdered. It was sad to me because the people who murdered the imam knew and understood his relationship to the Prophet. It is sad, because from that time to the present, people have been given the opportunity to choose a side. We can choose either to obey God and be with those who obey Him, or disobey God and be with those who disobey Him.

We all believe that we will make the right choice, but time has shown us over and over again that people continuously make the wrong decisions. Life has a way of taking our minds off of the prize, and that is preparing ourselves for what our eternal life is going to look like. It is sad to think about the family members who were left behind after the death of our imam, and the calamities they experienced. Visiting Imam Husayn, in particular, helped me personally to keep the reality of meeting our Lord near and dear to my heart.

The sadness felt after the first visit doesn't dissipate, but when I went and visited the shrine for the second time in 2017, I felt a great sense of empowerment born from that sadness. In my opinion, it puts our hardships in perspective, which allows us to recognize that no matter the hardships we may face, they will never be as tumultuous as those faced by Imam Hussayn, his family and his companions. My second trip was truly blessed and I was able to bring my phone into the shrine to take pictures and video and I also had the opportunity to interview with a TV station associated with the shrine. And for the second time, I had the honor of having lunch in a restaurant designated only for the visitors of Imam Hussayn.

I do want to take the time to say something here. It is always shocking, or rather, I found it shocking, that many people I had the opportunity to speak to were really surprised that

I am an African-American and I was there visiting the shrines. There's also a belief by some who are there that we absolutely have no knowledge. The looks on the faces of the people when you begin to relate to the story of Imam Husayn, or talk about how it is that you came into Islam, are priceless.

I don't think I mentioned up to this point how beautiful the shrines are. Aesthetically, they are very beautiful, and they give you a sense of wonderment. I believe that they are meant to be

beautiful to remind you of what heaven must be like. In Karbala, there are two shrines: one belonging to Imam Husayn and the other belonging to Abbas. I was told that the distance between the two shrines is the same as the distance between Safa and Marwah, the mountains in Mecca that the pilgrims run between to simulate how Haggar, the mother of Ishmael, ran back and forth from while she was looking for water for her son. Walking from one shrine to the other, I could feel a change in energy. I could feel my sense of sadness shift to anger as I walked from the shrine of Imam Hussayn to the shrine of Abbas. The people were mourning, but it almost felt like they were preparing. This man, Abbas, exemplified utter obedience and loyalty to his imam.

This was a man who was given the opportunity to walk away, to seek safety and save himself, but declined without hesitation. He chose to honor his commitment to God, and left this earthly plane as dedicated and steadfast in his

convictions as he had lived his entire life. He remained standing by his imam, his leader, and his brother, defending him until his last breath.

I had a very interesting experience while worshipping in this shrine. One night, when I couldn't sleep, I felt this overwhelming urge to go to the shrine to worship my Lord. It was about 3 a.m., and I went to the Shrine of Abbas and there weren't many people there. So, I grabbed a book of duas (supplications) and I began to read the Dua of Abu Hamza Thumali[16]. Here is how it starts,

> *O Allah: Do not discipline me by means of Your punishment*

إلهِي لا تُؤَدِّبْنِي بِعُقُوبَتِكَ

> *And do not subject me to Your planned strategy*

وَلا تَمْكُرْ بِي فِي حِيلَتِكَ

---

[16] The supplication of Abu Hamza al-Thumali, Abu Hamzah Al-Thumali, who was a companion of three Shia imams, received it from Ali Zayn al-Abidin (al-Sajad) and was the principal narrator of the work. This supplication is mentioned in Eqbal al-a'mal – a work in Arabic authored by Sayyed Ibn Tawus that included Du'as, prayers, and practices which were recommended to be performed at specific times of the year. It was said that Ali Zayn al-Abidin recited the supplication every evening or dawn during Ramadan.

How can I attain welfare, O Lord, while it is not found anywhere except with You?

مِنْ أَيْنَ لِيَ الْخَيْرُ يَا رَبِّ وَلا يُوجَدُ إلّا مِنْ عِنْدِكَ؟

And how can I find redemption while it cannot be attained save through You?

وَمِنْ أَيْنَ لِيَ النَّجَاةُ وَلا تُسْتَطَاعُ إلّا بِكَ؟

Neither he who has done righteous deeds can dispense with Your aid and mercy

لا الَّذِي أَحْسَنَ اسْتَغْنَى عَنْ عَوْنِكَ وَرَحْمَتِكَ

Nor can he who did evildoings, dare to challenge you and did not arrive at Your pleasure find an exit out of Your power

وَلا الَّذِي أَساءَ وَاجْتَرَأَ عَلَيْكَ وَلَمْ يُرْضِكَ خَرَجَ عَنْ قُدْرَتِكَ

While I was reading, two young men walked in and began to recite the story of Abbas. I was right next to the grave and as they began. One would recite, and the other would cry, and they would go back and forth. There were maybe about twenty to twenty-five people near the grave when they began; by the time they were midway through their recitation, there were hundreds of people. The story is very well known and the way that it is related is through chanting, for lack of a better term. I know that people don't like to hear the word singing, especially from the Islamic point of view, but it was like everyone was singing the same song and crying.

When you're in that place, nothing else matters. Time doesn't matter, because no matter what time you go, there are always people worshipping God. It's almost like there is a recharge to your life's batteries when you leave those places. We are inspired by these people's faith in God, and we begin to realize how thankful we should be for all the blessings that are bestowed upon us.

I had the opportunity to sit down with the administrators of both shrines. As I did at Imam Husayn's Shrine, I also had lunch at Abbas' Shrine. I was also given a gift; I received a ring that was made from the marble that was used on

Abbas' grave. The care that the individuals who keep the shrines beautiful and who see that visitors are taken care of has to be commended. They understand the duty that they have first and foremost towards their Lord. They also have to understand the emotional attachment that the individuals who come to visit have concerning those who they are visiting and their position with our Lord the Most High. This is a great responsibility, and from what I see, they take it very seriously.

Leaving Karbala was difficult and emotional for me and I was only comforted by the fact that I was headed back to Najaf.

SAMARA[17]

The next Holy City I visited was Samara. When I visited Iraq in 2013, I didn't have the opportunity to go to this beautiful place. At the time, it was very dangerous, and we had made a plan to go, but the night before we were

---

[17] Sāmarrā' is a city in Iraq. It stands on the east bank of the Tigris in the Saladin Governorate, 125 kilometers (78 mi) north of Baghdad. In 2003 the city had an estimated population of 348,700. In the medieval times, Samarra was the capital of the Abbasid Caliphate and the only remaining Islamic capital that retains its original plan, architecture and artistic relics. In 2007, UNESCO named Samarra one of its World Heritage Sites.

supposed to leave there was a bombing on the road. This shrine has a special place in my heart and in the heart of most Shia Muslims, and I will explain the reasoning behind it later.

Traveling to the shrine was really unnerving because of the scenery. Driving through the desert, you expect to see sand, but driving through the desert there, you see remnants of war. On the side of the road, you see abandoned tanks, Humvees and places that were under attack. The road was long and there wasn't a whole lot of different things to look at. As we got closer to the shrine, we began to encounter more and more checkpoints. This was different from both of the Holy Cities of Najaf and Karbala at this point, because those places had checkpoints, but not as many, and the people at the checkpoints weren't as intense. I later came to the understand that some of the last and fiercest fighting to remove Daesh (ISIS) happened in this area. So, they beefed up security and that was a good thing.

This shrine was under construction and it was not as big and polished as the other shrines that I had visited. The great dome was bombed in

2006, and the shrine was bombed again in 2007. I remember watching on the news and seeing images on social media of the rubble and destruction after the bombing. I remember feeling so bad and wanting to do something to try to defend that area. I was in Atlanta, Georgia and I had never visited Iraq; but I was reading about it, and trying to develop a relationship with Imam al-Hadi, Imam Hassan al-Askari, and of course Imam al-Mahdi, and I was devastated by the bombings. It was an empathic response that comes from having a relationship with someone or something.

Throughout their lifetimes, the imams from the Holy Household of the Prophet had difficult lives. The guardian of the shrine informed us that Imam al-Hadi was not allowed to go to Hajj. It was not like he was living under the rulership of non-Muslims. These were Muslims who did not allow the descendant and grandson of the Holy Prophet to make his obligatory Hajj. He stated that we, the believers, should sponsor people to go to Hajj on behalf of the imam and receive the blessings from doing so. When entering Samara, I saw the minaret of the great mosque of Samara. It is a beautiful piece of architecture and I can't lie, I really wanted to walk up to the top of it. This shrine was different, because it was not just the burial place for the imams, in fact, three of them called this place home, and the Imam of our Time was born here.

I mentioned that each shrine had a feel to it. The feeling that I had in this shrine was one of progression. There was a quietness about it and it felt majestic. I went downstairs to where Imam al-Mahdi grew up. Again, we read about things, but going to a place where people lived produces a different type of certainty. This place is special, and has that exceptional place in our hearts, because, as the guardian of the shrine so eloquently put it, "This place continues to be the

house of the Imam of our Time."

We went there and it was as if we were being hosted by the owner of the house. In a conversation, the guardian of the shrine made mention that they encourage people to not only come for visitation, but to also spend the night at the shrine, because there weren't any hotels or places to stay around. We ate lunch at the shrine, which was only afforded to a few people at the other shrines, but all the people who traveled to this shrine were also fed.

The hospitality that was shown was second to none. The commitment to rebuild and secure the safety of those who want to visit and worship at the shrine is unbelievable. I felt like the physical resurrection of the shrine is symbolic for the spiritual resurrection of the believers. The fact that such an important place for those who follow the faith is being restored, and made available to the believers to visit, should serve as a sign that we are making progress in this world. I find that it is something that is rarely mentioned but should be brought to the attention of believers around the world.

KADHIMIYAH[18]

The last shrine city I visited has a special importance for me. It is the birthplace of my

---

[18] Al-Kāẓimiyyah or al-Kāẓimayn is a northern neighborhood of the city of Baghdad, Iraq. It is about 5 kilometers (3.1 mi) from the city's center, on the west

teacher and the place where he grew up in the shade of Khadhimiyah. As soon as I arrived, my eyes locked in on the shrine, and I was overcome with emotions and could feel my heart filling with joy. The first thing that I wanted to do was to go and pray there, but before I could go there, I had to attend a meeting at the seminary. As was the case at the other seminaries, we were treated very well and were given the history of the seminary. I really enjoyed hearing about how the seminary began. This seminary was a satellite branch of Grand Ayatollah Sayyid Sistani's seminary in Najaf. One thing that I would like to mention here is that many of the seminary instructors and students were involved in liberating Iraq from oppression.

This shrine was different than all of the other shrines I had visited. The others were always open to visitors and this one was closed. I tried to get in to pray after the meeting was over, but I was unable to do so. That night when I went to sleep, I could feel myself tossing and turning. The goal is always to be in the physical proximity of God's most beloved. The extra bonus was for

---

bank of the Tigris. Al-Kāẓimiyyah is also the name of one of nine administrative districts in Baghdad. It is regarded as a holy city by Twelver Shi'ites.

me to pray in the places where my teacher prayed. I remember when Operation Desert Storm was going on in the early 90's and the news outlets talked about Baghdad. As a Muslim, you know that when a person isn't right, you have to stand against them. The news always talked about Baghdad and it being the place where Saddam was. What they never talked about was the spiritual significance and the individuals who were buried there. Although this place is in Baghdad, it is a city in itself and it is called Kadhimiyah. It was given this name because when Imam Musa al-Kadhim was buried, the people began to make pilgrimage to be near him, and to receive blessings for visiting God's most beloved. This imam lived a tumultuous life—he was arrested and put in prison many times—but never lost faith in his Lord. Each of the imams served as an example to all of us. We take lessons from their experiences and the stances they made throughout their lives. This story serves to show that not all of the imprisoned are actually criminals.

To me, it was absolutely amazing to visit the individual who, as a child, taught someone who is considered to be one of the foremost authorities on Islam. Abu Hanifa, who has a school of thought named after him, focused on the nature of accountability and sin. It was said that the imam was about five years old and Abu Hanifa asked him, "Does sin come from God or from the individual?" The imam stated that, "If the sin came from God, then God wouldn't have the right to punish you; if it was a partnership, then it would be unjust for the greater partner to punish the lesser in the partnership." He said, "Therefore, the sin has to come from the individual."

If a five-year-old were to deduce this today, he would be on every social media platform and labeled a boy genius. We honor these individuals, because despite the oppression that they received, they always lived their lives in the most exemplary of ways, allowing us to realize that following the laws and mandates of God is not impossible, even under the worst circumstances.

Along with visiting Imam Musa al-Kadhim, we also visited his grandson, Imam Muhammad al-Jawad, who is also buried there. As a young man, after his father Imam Ali al-Rida was murdered, he was summoned to Baghdad, where he had to go through a plethora of tests to prove that he had the knowledge to be the imam of the time. Being the most beloved of God was not a guarantee to having an easy life. Some of them went through unspeakable hardships; some of our imams lost their parents at an early age, not to mention that Prophet Muhammad was also an orphan, and God chose them to be our examples.

Anyone who knows me would tell you that I love taking pictures of all of the places that I have been. As soon as I saw this shrine, I immediately took a picture and sent it to my teacher and his son to show them that I finally made it to their hometown. This was special, because my teacher was one of the people who was tortured by Saddam, and was actually scheduled to be executed by him. But by the grace of God, my teacher avoided death and was given the ability to pour out his knowledge on us. I have no doubt that his being with us was due to him praying at those shrines, and I thank God for allowing me to go there and pray in the places where he prayed. My prayer is to be able to go back to Iraq with my teacher, so that we can worship at these holy places together, and thank God for the alliance that we have made.

For years, I read books, trying to gain an understanding of what Islam was truly about, and it was through this man, who grew up in the shade of the imams, that I truly gained a grasp of Islam and have been able to go all around the world to share the knowledge that he had imparted to me. The biggest blessing is that while I was in Iraq, I had the opportunity to share a lot of the Islamic knowledge taught to me by my teacher with others.

OTHER CITIES

Iraq is more than just a set of shrine cities. It has many other cities with hard-working citizens, and young people looking to build a better future. I was really impressed by the Iraqi people. What I witnessed in them was spirit of determination that has not been deterred despite their difficult circumstances. In Iraq, if you want to eat and have something in life, you have to earn it. This country has been involved in conflict after conflict. In this section, I want to talk about the other places I visited.

BAGHDAD[19]

When I was in Baghdad, we went to the headquarters of Al-Ayn Social Care Foundation, which is a charitable organization that was created to help the orphans of Iraq who were affected by all of the conflicts and terrorism that have occurred since 2006 in that country. I am a therapist and I have a master's degree in social work. I visited the headquarters of this organization with the preconceived notion that it would be somewhat disorganized, and not really equipped to help people, or make a difference. I assumed that they just put Band-Aids on situations, but I was so wrong.

When I was in London, I visited a branch of the organization there and saw the work being done, but I wasn't prepared to actually see how efficient and transparent this organization really is. In the building, there were clinics where people could seek treatment from physicians and dentists. There was an office dedicated to providing financial assistance for housing solutions for widows and orphans. The records

[19] Baghdad is the capital of Iraq. The population of Baghdad, as of 2016, is approximately 8,765,000, making it the largest city in Iraq, the second largest city in the Arab world (after Cairo, Egypt), and the second largest city in Western Asia (after Tehran, Iran).

were kept immaculately, and any individual making a donation from anywhere in the world could really see where their money was going and the impact it is making on the lives of those benefitting from it. Walking through the headquarters, we went to warehouses where clothing, bedding, toys, and furniture—to name a few of the things that are stored there—are made available for the orphans, widows and those who have been displaced because of armed conflict.

The thing that really surprised me was that people didn't have to go through hoops and hardships to receive help. The individuals filled out applications, showed that they were in need, a team was dispatched to confirm the data, and once the information was verified, they were given the help that they needed, as long as the supply was there. This is not a government organization. It is an organization that is supervised by the Grand Jurist, Ayatollah Sayyid Sistani. By no means is this a small operation, and what makes it so outstanding is the fact that the leader of this organization has the understanding that he is accountable to his Lord and Creator for doing what is right with the funds and resources that are under his control.

Here is a place that has had the unfortunate fate of being devastated by oppression and terrorism, and there was no relief, because insurgents came into the country and tried to destroy everything that was there. The Iraqi people did not fold and just give away what was theirs. They banded together, put their faith in God and gained victory!

Baghdad is a beautiful modern city. It is growing and hopefully will remain safe for people to come and visit, and see what was once a glorious place in the world. Hopefully this city can become associated with its spiritual past and disassociated with the bloody past created by Saddam.

BABYLON[20]

I went to Iraq during Christmas season. While I was there, I saw Christmas trees and Santa Claus, who they refer to as Baba Noel. I was raised as a

---

[20] Babylon was a key kingdom in ancient Mesopotamia from the 18th to 6th centuries BC. The city was built on the Euphrates river and divided in equal parts along its left and right banks, with steep embankments to contain the river's seasonal floods. Babylon was originally a small Akkadian town dating from the period of the Akkadian Empire c. 2300 BC.

Christian and I always had the impression that Iraq itself was Babylon, never realizing that Babylon was a city that has endured since ancient times in modern day Iraq. If you listen to the religious and political propaganda that is spouted about this place, you would think that only darkness can come from there. I am happy that I had the opportunity to go there, and to see things for myself, and to associate with the people.

My reasoning for going to Babylon at that time was because I was asked to visit some universities and religious seminaries on behalf of the office of Grand Ayatollah Sayyid Muhammad al-Hakim. His eminence was concerned about the youth in Iraq, especially those attending college. I was asked to go and speak to the students and faculty about my life and my journey to Islam.

The first place I went to visit was the University of Babylon. While I was touring the university, I was absolutely amazed by the technology and advancement of the students. They had state-of-the-art equipment and the latest technology to help the students achieve educational goals. I was amazed when I walked into a classroom which had a holographic heart, where, if you point a laser to any part, it would give you the name of the area, its function, and you could also feel the heart as it pumped in your hand through the laser device. In addition, something that was somewhat shocking was the fact that there were so many women attending the university. What the media would have you believe is that Muslim women in Islamic countries are not being educated, and are being oppressed. Clearly, this was not the case in this place, and there were women at all of the universities that I had the pleasure of visiting.

Something else that needs to be pointed out is that Christians also attended the universities. The Christians are able to practice their faith openly without any type of harassment. People of different faiths and schools of thought sat together, in the same classrooms, exchanged ideas, and also participated in each other's religious celebrations. The only thing I ever heard the news focus on concerning this country is the armed conflicts; they never talk about the importance that education plays in this country.

I was able to present at religious seminaries as well as universities where secular learning is taking place. I shared my story of being raised in a Christian home, where my mother and grandfather were both Christian ministers. I told them about the similarities between Christianity and Islam, and how there's very little separating the faiths. I mentioned how my need to worship God, in the way that He intended us to worship Him, drew me to Islam. People are who they are because of their parents and their environment. I felt it was crucial to have the individuals I addressed go back and look at the faith from the perspective of someone who was not raised in it. I asked them to do that because I did the same thing myself as a Christian before becoming a Muslim.

The most interesting and gratifying thing about presenting to the audience was having question-and-answer discussions with the students. It was so amazing to them that an American was there with them, and was able to discuss Islam at a high level, and answer many of their jurisprudential questions. I really enjoyed sharing with these young people and having them ask me about life in America, and to dispel many of the unfounded beliefs about living in the West. People who have never visited far off places and have only seen those places on TV believe that that is the reality, but in most cases, nothing could be further from that reality.

As I talked about issues in America, the students realized that these were the same issues they faced in their country. The students talked about not keeping pace with the rest of the world. Many of them talked about not having faith in the system that allowed fighting and having people of the same roots kill and oppress one another. I helped them to see that when the Europeans went to war, it was Christian against Christian in most cases, and that religion isn't the blame for things going wrong. Instead, the responsibility lies with those who practice the religion and their interpretation of whether or not they are doing what is right, or persist in doing what is wrong. I was able to remind them that the life of this world is temporary, and that God is just, and that every atom's weight of good will be given to those who do good, and every atom's weight of evil will be seen by those who do evil.

In all, I visited most of the institutions of higher learning while I was in Babylon, and I enjoyed every minute of it. My eyes were opened to a brand-new reality. There was a different feel in the cities. What I saw was real life, everyday people living and dealing with everyday life as residents in those cities, not just out-of-town visitors going to the shrine to pray. These were people who had regular jobs, children searching for the future and older people thinking about the days of yesterday, trying to figure out how to make the situation better for themselves and for future generations.

HILLAH[21]

Hillah is the place that I would love to invite all Christians and Jews to visit. I found this place to be beautiful and highly spiritual. Being raised as a Christian, many of the Bible stories take place in this area of the world, where the ancient city of Babylon once stood. I could have theoretically included this as one of the shrine cities but I didn't, because I believe that it would have taken

---

[21] Hillah is a city in central Iraq on the Hilla branch of the Euphrates River, 100 km (62 mi) south of Baghdad. The population is estimated at 364,700 in 1998. It is the capital of Babylon Province and is located adjacent to the ancient city of Babylon, and close to the ancient cities of Borsippa and Kish.

away from it being the historical location that it is. I guess I will start from the earliest people, and move forward as far as what I had the opportunity to experience while being in Hillah.

I had the honor of visiting the birthplace of the father of the monotheistic faiths, Prophet Abraham. Many people don't realize that there is a similarity between Moses, Jesus, and the twelfth Imam of Shia Islam. The similarity is that each of them lived at a time that had a corrupt ruler who was informed that a reformer was to be born in their kingdom who would later come to destroy them. The pregnancy of Abraham's mother was concealed and he was born in a cave. I had the opportunity of going into that cave and praying there.

What is amazing is that around this area, sheep were grazing, there were open fields, people walking around in traditional dress, and it was as if I was taken back in time to a far distant place. Right outside the place where Abraham was born are ruins from the time of King Nimrod. It was such a blessing to walk to places that I had read about when I was a child. Never in my wildest dreams did I think I would have the opportunity to go and visit this place, and what was more amazing was how the people treated these places and kept them intact for future generations.

Every Sunday school student can tell you about Nebuchadnezzar. We read about Daniel and the lion's den, and I was right in the area where all of that took place. But what was more remarkable to me was having the opportunity to go to a temple that Ezekiel from the Bible built. The Jews in the area, along with the Muslims, have kept this place intact. Actually, while I was there the first time, they were restoring it and you could actually see the Hebrew writing on the walls. Again, reading the Bible and knowing that the children of Israel were taken from their homeland and brought to Babylon is something that is well known. What is not well known is that these individuals were allowed to worship and actually had a place of worship that is still in existence today. Just thinking about Iraq, it has the who's who of Biblical Prophets who lived and are buried there.

I would not be just if I did not talk about Prophet Ayyub, otherwise known as Job. Again, growing up as a Christian and being a child who attended Sunday school, I definitely learned about Job. When it comes to trials and tribulations, people generally refer back to Job especially, in terms of not turning away from faith. We all have our trials and tribulations, but we don't go through the things that Job did. In the Holy Quran, God talks about mankind being tested with loss of wealth, materials, children and health. Job experienced all of these things and was constantly told by his friends and neighbors to curse God and die for having to go through all of those trials. But Job didn't do it. He continued to have faith in God, and after he completed his test, God restored back to him what he had lost.

There is a well, from which God told Job to use the water to bathe in, and after he did, he was healed. As Job began to wash with the well water, the sores that he had on his body began to heal, and his physical restoration was complete. I had the opportunity to use that water, and I'll talk about what I believe it meant for me a little later on in this book. People from all over the world come to this well and drink from it and take water with them, and they report being healed of their ailments after drinking it. There's a wall where people write their names as a testament for being healed of the ailments after drinking the water. God willing, when I return, I will add my name on to that wall.

Also in Hillah is the grave of Qasim, the son of Imam Musa al-Kadhim, and the brother of Imam Ali ar-Ridha. Although this isn't the imam himself, he was deeply loved by his father and his brother, who were both imams. I had the opportunity to go to his shrine, and when you enter, there is a statement and prayer from Imam Ali ar-Ridha. In the prayer, he asked that all of the people who wanted to visit him and didn't have the means or ability to visit him, God will bless those who visited his brother with the blessings as if they came to visit him. Throughout the ages, how important has this blessing been? It may be a bigger blessing today in light of the current political landscape. This place was immaculate and very well kept and had a very peaceful feel to it.

As someone who grew up as a Christian, I can really appreciate and have a great deal of respect for the people of this area. They have taken the time to ensure that these historical sites are maintained and available for people to visit. What is interesting is that no one has to pay for admission, there are no ropes around the building prohibiting people from going in. These places are open, clean, and no-one is harassed. You can go in and worship and come out feeling renewed and spiritually cleansed. This area connects with me and as I think about it now, it brings tears to my eyes, because I wasn't reading about a fairy tale: I was reading about actual people who lived in actual places, and had trials and tribulations like everyone else. These individuals are inspirational, because, despite all that they endured, they made a decision to serve God, and God has honored them by ensuring that their history and their memory is preserved so that people to this day can visit, remember, and reflect on their exemplary lives. It is almost like the preservation of Pharaoh, but in this case, it is to show righteousness, not disobedience. God says: "Go throughout the Earth and see what happened to those who came before you." During that visit, I was able to see that.

NASRIYAH[22]

I was scheduled to go to Basra to meet with a group of professors, and on the way there, we stopped in Nasriyah, where there is an Islamic seminary. While traveling on the highway to this town, I was reminded of how dangerous this country had been. No one was exempt from being targeted by the insurgents who came into this country. While driving there, I saw a bus that was blown up on the side of the road. It was a school bus. I was told that a suicide bomber drove through a checkpoint while a bus near it was taking little children to school. He detonated a bomb, killing himself and all the children onboard the bus. Everything takes on a different perspective when thinking that at any time, and at any place, someone would be callous enough to blow themselves up and everyone that is around them—it is beyond my comprehension. As a Muslim, I know that this is not a part of the religion, and it is a shame that people who do these types of things try to associate themselves with the faith.

---

[22] Nasiriyah is a city in Iraq. It is situated along the banks of the Euphrates River, about 225 miles (370 km) southeast of Baghdad, near the ruins of the ancient city of Ur. It is the capital of the Dhi Qar Governorate. Its population 2003 was about 560,000, making it the fourth largest city in Iraq.

When we entered the town, I was taken to the local mosque that houses the seminary and I gave a presentation. One thing I think I failed to mention was that in all of the universities or seminaries I visited, the people couldn't wait to take pictures with me. These young men and women talked about wanting to follow me on social media to learn from me, and to see what I was doing in my life. They made it clear that I was an inspiration for them because I had access to everything that was glorified, and turned away from it. They recognized that there was nothing stopping me from drinking, smoking, fornicating, and excessive living, and yet, I accepted Islam and chose to live a righteous life. They could see that their fantasies were all at my fingertips, but I decided, like so many other Americans did, to turn away from those things when they were readily accessible. Their faces lit up with hope and many of them decided to reaffirm their faith and rededicated their lives to learning more about their religion, and how it changed the lives of those whom it was improbable to reach.

After finishing the program, I was invited to visit the local school. The schools there resembled schools that existed in the States a long time ago; students of all grades, from first grade to graduation, attended the same school. The people of the town were so proud of this school, because they built and financed it themselves. Again, this isn't like living in the United States, where we take education for granted. Those people had to come up with their own money, because no one was going to educate their children; so, they found a way to educate their children themselves. This is what I was referring to when I talked about the Iraqi people having a spirit of determination.

I was also taken to a site where they were building houses for widows and orphans. The people were building homes from the ground up to ensure that individuals who lost their homes in the conflict had a place to stay. The houses were being supplemented by donations from Muslim scholars. The people don't have the government to rely on to feed them or to house them. They have to make their own way and they are doing it. Here I thought that I was going to inspire people, but in the end, I was being inspired.

These people, many of whom had very little means, created businesses for themselves to survive. They would make towing vehicles by putting a wooden box that resembled a truck bed on their motorcycles and use it to carry things or remove rubble to support themselves. Some of them would sell gas in jars on the side of the road, make bricks, or do whatever they had to do to support themselves and their families. When people tell me now that they can't start, build and maintain a community in the States, I am going to tell them about the Iraqi people, and see if they can inspire them the way that they inspired me.

I didn't mention this earlier, but I need to mention it here—a feast was prepared everywhere I went. No matter what these people's problems or worries were, they pulled together to make me, a stranger, feel comfortable. This is Islamic hospitality! It is also something that is rarely talked about when people mention the faith of Islam. I truly enjoyed myself, and before leaving that city, I went to the mosque, Masjid Fatima Zahra, and had a conversation with seminary students and community members. The question and answer sessions of all the talks that I had were very enlightening and informative from both sides.

The best questions I had from all of the schools revolved around the issue of "How do we keep our children interested in faith?" What is amazing about that question is that it is the same exact question that I am asked in the UK, America, and Canada. I always give the same answer: "The way to keep the children interested in our faith is to make it relevant to our time." I let them know that we have to show how faith is viable and has solutions to the problems that we are facing today, and that it is not an old relic that should be placed in a corner somewhere.

BASRA[23]

The last city I visited was Basra, which is located in the south of Iraq. I left Nasriyah and stayed the night in Basra. When I woke up, we had tea and left the house to go to al-Ahwar[24], The

---

[23] Basra is an Iraqi city located on the Shatt al-Arab between Kuwait and Iran. It had an estimated population of 2.5 million in 2012. Basra is also Iraq's main port, although it does not have deep water access, which is handled at the port of Umm Qasr.

[24] The Ahwar of Southern Iraq: Refuge of Biodiversity and the Relict Landscape of the Mesopotamian Cities is a UNESCO World Heritage Site located in south Iraq. The Ahwar currently consists of seven sites, including three cities of Sumerian origin and four wetland areas of the Mesopotamian Marshes: Huwaizah Marshes,

Marshlands. I learned a lot that day. I learned that Iraq was not one big desert, but that it had many different environments. We went to the marsh and I saw jamoos, also known as water buffalos. It was incredible to see children walking next to the humongous beasts and not being afraid. I had the privilege of getting into a boat and traveling through the marsh. While in the boat, I received an education about this beautiful place. I was told that Saddam had drained most of the water from the marsh, and it considerably changed the habitat and waterscape there. I found it very interesting that the last city I visited gave me the most lasting and evident example of how ruthless and heartless Saddam really was.

A building was erected on the marsh, dedicated to the martyrs who were killed by Saddam while trying to liberate Iraq from his oppression. Despite being drained by Saddam, the marsh remains the largest in that area of the world, and it continues to benefit the people and animals who live there. It is home to many different species of plant life and animals. People even

---

Central Marshes, East Hammar Marshes, West Hammar Marshes, Uruk Archaeological City, Ur Archaeological City, and Tell Eridu Archaeological Site.

lived on the marsh in huts. When I returned to the house where I was staying, we had breakfast that featured cheese and yogurt made from water buffalo milk. Never in my life did I ever think that I would have eaten that. Again, I was a stranger and people opened up their homes, provided me with a place to rest and gave me nourishment.

The highlight of my trip to Basra was going to the mosque were Imam Ali was when he first came to Iraq. One of the walls from the fort that existed when the imam was there was still standing and the mosque was in the middle. I began my journey visiting Imam Ali in Najaf, and I ended up at the Imam Ali Masjid (mosque) in Basra. I can't verbalize the feeling I had being there. Again, to walk into places where my heroes walked, and more importantly to worship in the places that they worshipped, is far beyond anything that I could have ever imagined. I am an African American man from Savannah, Georgia, who wasn't even born in the religion of Islam, but has traveled to one of the holiest places on Earth simply because I said, "God is my Lord."

My last stop before leaving Basra was to meet a group of professors from the university. I met with them in an Islamic center that was created in the community where they lived from one of the units that was not being inhabited. Being with those educated men was definitely a blessing, and having the opportunity to talk about the impact of faith in the lives of students was exhilarating and satisfying.

Driving back to the Holy City of Najaf from Basra is a five-hour trip. We traveled back late at night and in the distance, I could see where the oil refineries were, because I could see the fire rising from them. There wasn't a whole lot of scenery or many street lights. This gave me the opportunity to really reflect on my trip and how blessed I was to be able to visit the most beloved of our Lord, the Most High! The thing that is most salient to me is the sense that people are all the same, with many of the same concerns. In that country, you have people who are very rich, who enjoy all the modern conveniences that can be found anywhere in the world, and you have poor people who, if not for the mercy of others, will die of starvation. This is the same anywhere you go.

I talked to people in the shrine cities, many who have lost their faith, who don't go to the shrines to pray, and who only have words of complaint towards religious people and their scholars. I also talked to people who lost their faith but came back to it and could never imagine leaving it again. Living in a certain place or being from a particular family does not exempt people from being subjected to life's trials and tribulations, this is true anywhere in the world, and this place is definitely not exempt. All we could do is what we were created to do, and to follow the example of those who did it best, and that is to worship our Lord. It doesn't matter if we have an easy life or a turbulent one, we all belong to God and to God we must return.

PREPARATION

I have come to the conclusion that my blessing of being able to go to Iraq was so that I could be prepared for future life-changing events. When I went to Iraq in 2013, I had a wonderful trip, but I wasn't prepared for what was going to happen later that year. From the time I came home to the end of 2013, it seemed like I was always attending funerals. Life teaches us that we all belong to God and we all have to return to Him. There's no mystery in that system. We are born and we are going to die. We all try to prepare ourselves, and live the lives we need to live so that our afterlife is in close proximity to our Lord. We know that death is inevitable and we hear about people dying every day. You would think that we would become emotionally immune and desensitized when hearing about death, because we hear about it all the time. But God allowed us to build attachments with people, and when our loved ones die, we feel it deeply, and it hurts.

2013 was a dark year for me, because I lost a few relatives, but what impacted me most was losing my grandmother. As I'm writing, tears are falling from my eyes. Of all the people in the world, my grandmother was the one who believed that I could accomplish anything in life. She was by far my biggest supporter. She and my grandfather were my anchors! They were the ones who showed me what it meant to be a true believer in God, and to hold on to my faith in Him.

To add to that, I lost my nephew a few days after losing my grandmother. My grandmother and my nephew died a few days apart and they were buried a few days apart.

Going to Iraq in general, and specifically going to Karbala, really gave me the strength to maintain my faith and to make it through that stressful time. I often thought about how much the family of the Prophet had to go through, and how they were able to maintain their faith through all of the traits and tribulations. I knew that my examples would pull me through. Being in Iraq helped me to remember that none of us are exempt from having to taste death, as God promised us in the Quran.

There was a burning in my soul when I first heard my grandmother died, but as the tears rolled down my face, I was reminded that we are all going to have to make that same journey, and that success at the end of the journey is being the best and most obedient servants that we can possibly be. I was reminded that death isn't the end, although some have you believe that it is. I understood that it truly is the beginning of what will be our eternal existence.

I have seen people who have become mentally unstable, or who have gone into deep depressions after losing a loved one. The examples I had of people losing loved ones in a more horrific way than I did are the members of the Prophet's Household, and because of their faith, I knew that I was going to be alright and eventually I was. All praises belong to God.

My trip to Iraq in 2017 to 2018 was another time of preparation. Of course, I didn't go into the trip with that in mind, but not too long after I returned, I began to understand that it was. I talked about what happened to me while I was preparing to go, and what happened to me immediately after I arrived in Iraq. What I didn't talk about was what happened to me immediately after I came home. I began a new job a few days after I came back to the States.

I was riding really high and preparing to do a lot of different things. I had just made the journey of a lifetime, for the second time, and I was feeling very inspired. I completed a life-coaching course to go along with my clinical training. My faith was at an all-time high. I just knew that there was nothing that was going to stop me from achieving everything that I set my mind to.

But prior to me leaving Iraq, my stomach began to run and I had a bad case of diarrhea and gas. I came home and thought that it was something that would pass, but it didn't. I found myself in excruciating pain for more than a month, and it affected my ability to work and enjoy life. I went to my doctor a few times and asked if there was something he could do, but there was nothing.

Finally, on Valentine's Day, I went to dinner and afterwards I felt so bad that I tried a home remedy to try to deal with my aching belly. I drank some baking soda and water in hopes of relieving my gas. It was the worst thing that I could have done, or at least I thought it was, so I went to the emergency room and I was admitted into the hospital. The doctors did a CAT scan and saw that there was nothing moving through my colon. At that point, no water, no air, nothing was moving and I was feeling miserable.

I remained in the hospital for two weeks while my doctors were figuring out the best course of action for treating me. I probably could have been in and out of the hospital within a few days because the surgeon wanted to operate a day or two after I came in, but the gastrointestinal doctors thought that they could clear the blockage without surgery.

Here I was, freshly back from being in Iraq, having prayed at all the shrines and asked for intercession from our Lord's most beloved. I never had doubts in my mind, but I began to think that maybe me going over there was preparing me for this ordeal that I was going through now. As time went by, I went downstairs to the gift shop and bought a journal so that I could record my thoughts. I was thinking to myself that I could use this as a testimony and show everyone how my faith in God pulled me through, and thinking that once this was over, everything would be great.

I talked to my parents. My mother, step-father and sister drove up from Savannah to be with me. My stepfather and my sister went back to Savannah and my mother stayed while I was having the surgery, and that was a great comfort. My doctor let me know before the surgery that there was a possibility that I would have to wear a colostomy bag right after the surgery. I wasn't too happy about that, but what was I going to do? I prayed the night before the surgery and continued to ask for intercession. The next morning, I went to have surgery and the surgery lasted a lot longer than they had expected.

I was told that I was so impacted that it took a while for them to remove all the blockage from my body. The surgeon removed eight inches from my colon. I woke up and I had a hole in my stomach and a bag over it. I remember a nurse coming in to show me how to clean my colostomy. This was strange, but in life, you have to do what you have to do, and that's the only choice you really have. It took me a little while to perfect putting that bag on, but once I got it, I had it. But there was something else going on too!

I have a disease called sarcoidosis. It is an autoimmune disease, and I was taking prednisone to help with the symptoms. While I was in Iraq, I prayed to have that disease cured and removed from me. While I was in the hospital, the doctor said that my health was great and if they hadn't known that I had a blockage in my colon, they would have sent me home. I was instructed not to take prednisone, and I have not taken it since. I thought to myself that the worst was behind me, that I had passed my test and that would be all.

Little did I know, there was something else brewing. I was scheduled to have my second surgery in May of 2018, to reconnect my colon so that I would no longer have to wear a colostomy bag. I was really riding high, because my daughter was graduating with an associate's degree in psychology. At the same time, she was graduating high school with her diploma, which was a great accomplishment. We were planning to have a big celebration for her, and all of my family would come and celebrate with us. It was around this time that I found out that my father was sick. We found out that he had cancer, but they didn't know what stage the cancer was in, and they didn't know exactly what type of cancer he had. It was rough, but we live in a time of great medicine and modern technology and people are surviving cancer every day. My father was a strong person. He was exercising three to four times a week, if not more, he was eating right, and doing the things that he needed to do to live his best life. A few weeks later, they found out that he was in stage four, and a few weeks after that, they diagnosed him with stomach cancer. They told us he only had a few weeks to live.

I wasn't ready for this. I never saw it coming! I thought my testing and my trials were already behind me, but they were just about to begin. My stepmother, my sisters and I all worked hard to try to keep my father in good spirits and do the things that we needed to do for him to be comfortable. We comforted one another and it helped a lot. My father died around the beginning of Muharram. I knew that I could not go out and give lectures during that time, because it would have just been too much. I was asked to do a house lecture (majlis) for someone, and because of my relationship with them, I agreed. I gave my lecture from the perspective of the son who lost his father, Imam Zainul Abedin. It gave me a brand-new perspective, and a different way to look at the tragedy that occurred in Karbala.

Sometimes you can look at a situation, see it, read it, talk about it, ponder over it, and walk away feeling okay about it. But this time, having lost my father and lived through that experience changed everything. My journey to Iraq helped to prepare me to be the patriarch of my family now, in the same way that Imam Ali Zainul Abedin had to be. Now I am responsible for my stepmother, sisters, nieces and nephews. Those are big shoes to fill that my dad left for me, but being in the presence of God's most beloved gave me the fortitude to be able to fill those shoes and take up the mantle that I needed to take up.

I continue to pray that I am able to go back to visit Iraq. I don't want to have to prepare for another death, but it doesn't matter if I go or not, because death is the reality. We all belong to God and to God we must return. Going over there helps to prepare us not only for the death of our loved ones, but most importantly, for our own deaths. It makes us realize that this life isn't promised to be ours forever and that the time we have should not be taken for granted or wasted. So, I implore myself first, and anyone who may read this, to always be mindful of your duty to your Lord, the Most High. After all, He says: "The greatest among you are those who have the greatest taqwa [awareness of God]!"

INSPIRATION

While I was in Iraq, I always took the opportunity to record my feelings. I wrote a few things while I was there and I would like to share them here as a form of inspiration. Some were written while I was leaving, and others were written when I was there. I hope and I pray that this offering helps someone decide that they want to make a visit to Iraq, or more importantly, to get their lives in line with the will of God. I pray that the Lord watches you, keeps you, and allows you to fulfill all of your legitimate desires.

PONDERING

Just pondering about the visitation. "Why do people go on Ziyarat (the visitation)? Some people go so that they can say, "I have gone to this place." Others go so that they can belong to an exclusive group, those who have gone to visit the saints of God. Why would a person like me want to go to Iraq? I don't have a family connection there, I can barely speak the language, and the country is in shambles because of the wars it has endured over the past few decades.

This place doesn't normally turn up in your top five destinations for vacation; however, millions of people flock to it on a yearly basis, and participate in the world's largest peaceful gathering.

The hotel accommodations are not always the greatest and, in many cases, the Wi-Fi is bad. You're probably not going to have a lot of opportunities to have five-star dining either. Some of the buildings are dilapidated, the roads are unfinished and riding around the city in a taxi is a very scary situation. Yet, despite all of that, people still come and stay in places that they would not spend good money to stay in if they were in the States, eat food that they wouldn't buy, and walk dusty roads, and all for what?

The answer is that it is all about the connection! It is taking the time to connect with the individuals who understood the purpose of life. It is to feel close to those who believed in justice, equality, and existing with others in peace and harmony. It is about being close to those who lived out: "Be truthful even if you have to bear witness against yourself!"

It is understanding that the visitations to these holy places don't begin when we get there, but that they began when we have built a connection by learning about these selfless individuals, who gave their lives to make sure that we would have the opportunity to worship God in the way that He wants us to worship Him! It is knowing that when things get hard, decisions are tough, and success is highly unlikely, that we have examples of people who cared more about their souls than they did about worldly gains.

Oh Iraq, what your sands have witnessed!

The treasures that are buried within them and the blood of those whom God has purified. This is why we come!

We want to connect with those who have the strongest connection with God! To be with the most beloved removes the fear of danger, war, and death. It compels us to forgo life's luxuries, to sit with saints. It humbles us to see people who have less than we have, who have experienced more trauma than we have, who give their last to show hospitality to those who have come to visit God's most beloved! Proud people who rub feet and give rest to those walking for miles to be with God's saints.

When asked, "Why go to this war-torn place?"

I simply answer,

> It is the birthplace of Abraham.
>
> It is the place where God cured Job!
>
> It is the place where Daniel was protected from the lions in the lion's den.
>
> It is the place where a man died in the best of positions, with his head on the ground, worshipping his Lord!
>
> It is the place where this same man, after being struck, proclaimed, 'By the Lord of the Kaaba, I have gained success.'

It is the place where humanity was placed on notice when Imam Husayn said, "Is there anyone to help me?"

We come here screaming, answering his call. We are here to stand as he did against tyranny and we stand with him in our obedience to God!

Oh God raise us with those we love for Your sake!

THE POWER OF PRAYER

My Grandmother used to sing,

> *Somebody prayed for me, had me on their mind, took their time and for me!*
>
> *I'm so glad they prayed...*
>
> *I'm so glad they prayed for me!*

I grew up understanding the power of prayer, and have witnessed miracles in my life, and in the lives of others through the power of prayer. But what is that power?

The true power of prayer is having the faith before you go before the Almighty that your prayers are going to be answered.

The power of prayer is believing that when you ask people to intercede with God on your behalf, when we ask, "Please pray for me," that God loves to hear our needs from tongues that are not ours, and He is willing to accept the intercession, but we have to believe.

The power of prayer is knowing that we serve a God with whom everything is possible!

With belief and trust in this fact, doubts and insecurities find no place in the hearts of the believers.

Sometimes when our prayers are not answered, it's because it may not be your season, or what you've asked for is not in your best interest, or sometimes because we doubted and did not exercise our faith in God, and therefore negated the power of prayer.

The highest level of faith is certainty!

First, we submit, then we believe, we become sincere in that belief, and then we become unshakable, immovable, and truly certain in the

power of God! That's why the faithful prosper:
they understand the power of prayer!

SAYING GOODBYE

O' Iraq, I wasn't impressed with you when we first met. You were so dusty and full of rubble. Guns and guards were at every checkpoint, making me feel like a prisoner. I only felt free when I first saw the Shrine of Imam Ali—after that, you removed your veil and showed your true self.

Your sands are filled with the wisdom of the Prophets, and the blood of the martyrs. You showed me why you are part of what is called the Fertile Crescent. I look at my shoes and refuse to clean them, because I want to keep your sand and dust there to remind me of you. This, my love, isn't goodbye. It is peace until we meet again.

> *Salaams[25] to all of you Prophets of God.*
>
> *Salaams to you, O' Imams of the Blessed House.*
>
> *Salaams to you, all of the faithful companions.*
>
> *Salaams to you, all of the martyrs of God.*
>
> *And Salaam to you, O' Land of Iraq.*

---

[25] Peace.

THE AUTHOR

Paul McCoy is a mental and behavioral health specialist who is a licensed master social worker, chaplain and life coach. He currently works with veterans, prisoners, and families who have issues ranging from domestic violence to substance abuse. Mr. McCoy uses many modalities to help the individuals that he sees including the principles of Islam to help the individuals through the trying times. Mr. McCoy is also a lecturer and author who has written on many subjects including comparative religion.

Made in the USA
Las Vegas, NV
26 September 2023